Emeril

20-40-60

Also by Emeril Lagasse

· ·

Emeril

20–40–60

FRESH FOOD FAST

Emeril Lagasse

WITH PHOTOGRAPHY BY STEVEN FREEMAN

harperstudio

An Imprint of HarperCollins*Publishers*

EMERIL 20–40–60. Copyright © 2009 by Emeril/MSLO Acquisition Sub, LLC. All rights reserved. Printed in the United States of America. No part of this book may be used or reproduced in any manner whatsoever without written permission except in the case of brief quotations embodied in critical articles and reviews. For information address HarperCollins Publishers, 10 East 53rd Street, New York, NY 10022.

HarperCollins books may be purchased for educational, business, or sales promotional use. For information please write: Special Markets Department, HarperCollins Publishers, 10 East 53rd Street, New York, NY 10022.

For more information about this book or other books from HarperStudio, visit www.theharperstudio.com.

FIRST EDITION

Designed by Leah Carlson-Stanisic

Library of Congress Cataloging-in-Publication Data has been applied for.

ISBN 978-0-06-174294-1

09 10 11 12 13 WBC/RRD 10 9 8 7 6 5 4 3 2 1

This book is for all my wonderful fans,

you terrific home cooks out there who keep me
inspired and keep me going. Thanks for sticking
by me. I hope the recipes within these pages help
make your lives a little less hectic and a whole
lot tastier. (Remember, it's all about food of love.)

TRI-PLY CLAD CONSTRUCTION

Emeril
PRO-CLAD™
2 CUP/0.5 QT

Contents

Acknowledgments

Emeril 20–40–60 would never have made it to the table on time without the help of everyone below—

My amazing family, who is always, always there for me—Alden, EJ, Meril, Jessie, Jillian, Mom, Dad, Mark, Wendi, Katti Lynn, Dolores, Jason, and baby Jude. I love you all.

My incredible Culinary team who always make it happen against all odds—Charlotte Martory, Alain Joseph, Stacey Meyer, Angela Sagabaen, and Kamili Hemphill. Two down, eight to go!

My supportive Homebase team—Eric Linquest, Tony Cruz, Dave McCelvey, Marti Dalton, Chef Chris Wilson, Chef Bernard Carmouche, Chef Dana D'Anzi, Tony Lott, Scott Farber, and George Ditta.

Photographer Steven Freeman and his on-the-ready photography associates, Kevin Guiler and Josh Maready.

My associates at Martha Stewart Living Omnimedia—Martha, Charles, Robin, Lucinda, and the hospitable test kitchen staff.

My super M's—Mara Warner Jones, Michelle Terrebonne, and Maggie McCabe.

Mimi Rice Henken and TJ Pitre, for their assistance with the photo shoot and photo editing.

The very talented design team who made the photos come alive—Jed and Elias Holtz and Charissa Melnik.

My pal, Sal Passalacqua.

Shelley Van Gage, for helping me look my best.

Our partners at HarperStudio, for their vision—Bob Miller, Debbie Stier, Sarah Burningham, Julia Cheiffetz, Katie Salisbury, Sally McCartin, Jacqui Daniels, Mary Schuck, Leah Carlson-Stanisic, Kim Lewis, Lorie Young, Nikki Cutler, Doug Jones, Kathie Ness, and Ann Cahn.

Our partners at All-Clad, T-Fal, and Wusthof.

My friends at Leonard Simchick Prime Meats and Fresh Poultry and at Pisacane Fish Market—you guys are the best.

All the terrific employees at my restaurants and Homebase who make it happen every day.

My dear friends Frank and Richard Santorsola.

Sherif, for getting me where I need to go each and every day.

Jim Griffin, my terrific agent and friend.

My friend and trusted counsel, attorney Mark Stein.

Thank you all from the bottom of my heart.

FRESH FOOD FAST: IT'S AS EASY AS 1–2–3

Is this world getting faster? More and more folks are asking me the same question these days: "Emeril, how can I find the time to prepare exciting meals at home without sacrificing quality? How do you do it?" They tell me that with the passing of each year, there's less time available. Even with all the new technology that's supposed to simplify our lives, we're pulled in a thousand directions. And when children are involved in the equation—forget it! There's always a soccer game to be played, homework to be done, questions that need to be answered, and visits to the gym (we have to keep our "machines" running smoothly!). I'm sure you get the picture—because, trust me, these folks aren't telling me anything that I don't live myself 365 days a year. But I honestly do believe that with a few basic principles under the belt and a fresh mind-set, anyone is capable of putting delicious, well-balanced meals on the table in the time they have available. And that, my friend, is the philosophy behind this book:

Make the meals you want in the time you have.

To help you kick things up and simplify your life all at the same time, I've collected close to 160 recipes here, from startlingly simple ones that can be ready in next to no time, to some more lavish recipes that might take a bit of time to simmer but that are still a cinch to put together. The recipes are divided into three basic categories: The 20-minute chapter is comprised of dishes that can be on the table in 20 minutes or less; the 40-minute chapter is for dishes that fall between 20 and 40 minutes (with many of them hovering around the 30-minute mark); and the 60-minute chapter is peppered with a few special recipes that can take anywhere from 40+ to 60+ minutes to get to the table. While these longer "splurge" recipes may seem "time-luxurious," they can still be perfect for a not-so-hectic weekday, a lazy Sunday afternoon, or an end-of-the-week meal. You know what time you have. Be honest with yourself and you're on your way to making this collection of recipes work for you.

In cooking quick, fresh meals at home, there are many steps we can take to make the process easier than we had imagined:

Read the recipe(s) from beginning to end once you've decided what you want to cook. This can be done anytime—on a lunch break during the day or even during your daily commute (riding, not driving!). The point is that at some time before you actually start cooking, you need to have an idea of what you'll be doing. Take a few minutes and run things through in your mind, visualizing the ingredients called for and the steps you will take to prepare each dish. This way, when you actually begin to cook, there are no surprises and you're ready to go. Practicing this kind of methodical thinking will become second nature and will transform you into a speed demon in the kitchen!

Ready to begin? **Read through the recipe (again) and gather all of your ingredients and equipment**. You'll spare yourself from going back and forth, making prep time a breeze. Also, make a note to yourself if you notice a task in the recipe that can be tackled while doing something else. For example, zero in on inactive time. Inactive time in the kitchen basically refers to time that does not require your full attention, such as waiting for something to marinate, bringing a liquid to a boil, or finishing something in the oven. **Be smart and use that time wisely** to do other things, such as finishing prep (like chopping herbs or grating cheese for a garnish), beginning another recipe, or catching up on tasks around the house (what's that, dirty dishes in the sink?). This way once dinner is on the table, you're free to sit and enjoy with friends and family.

Keep a well-stocked pantry at all times, so you're ready when the hunger hits. While fresh is my preference when available and when it's in season, there are certain packaged items that I always have on hand, such as pasta, rice, canned beans, and tomatoes, just to name a few. You know what you like. I also think of my **freezer** as a friend in creating fresh food fast, since many things do just fine in the freezer for short periods of time. These things come in handy when going to the store isn't an option. **Frozen vegetables and fruits are often** examples of produce that were picked and quickly processed at the peak of ripeness, making these a better option than off-season, pricey supermarket finds that traveled way too far. A small package of nuts kept in the freezer, defrosted and quickly toasted, can be just the added note a salad needs. A well-wrapped loaf of day-old French bread freezes well, too, and can quickly be transformed into tasty croutons to really make that soup or salad sing. And hey, don't forget about your biggest ally—your **fridge**. Keep yours well stocked with prewashed greens and other produce that will help get you through your week, along with the dairy basics and your personal favorite condiments. Hey, what are those door shelves for, anyway? With a little **prior proper planning** (the three Ps, as I like to call it), you're on your way to an impromptu meal in no time.

Fresh herbs rule! Though we use many dried herbs and seasonings in the recipes in this book, since that is what many cooks typically have on hand, if you have a little green space out back or a roomy kitchen window, I would suggest keeping a few pots of herbs going year-round. Fresh herbs are quick to snip when needed and add an unmistakable touch to any dish. My kids love watering the herbs at the end of the day—it's one of the fun things that we do together, making them feel more connected to the cooking process, too.

Multitasking is important in the home kitchen, too, just like we cooks do in the restaurant kitchens. For example, if you need to mince some garlic for tonight's dinner, make a little extra (or lagniappe, as we say here in New Orleans) for tomorrow's feast. You can also do the same for chopping onions and scallions. Just reserve them in airtight containers and store them in the refrigerator for up to 4 days. You can apply the same idea when cooking pasta or rice: make a little extra, save yourself some time, and have it ready for another night's dinner. You might decide to turn these items into a delicious salad or add them to a brothy soup. It's just good kitchen economics. I also make **stocks in big batches** when I have the time, often utilizing the carcasses of roasted poultry from previous meals, and then freeze the stock in small portions for later. And of course, with a little creative thinking, leftover roast poultry, meats, and roasted or grilled veggies can come together to create fabulous sandwiches, salads, pastas, and risottos.

But, you know, whether speaking of ingredients available or of time on hand, in the end, it's all about doing the best with what you have and enjoying yourself along the way. Everyone's lives are different, so I've given you many options here. Whether you have 20 minutes, 40 minutes, or 60 minutes to put a meal together, and whether you're prepared because you've stocked your pantry well, kept some tasty leftovers to use in a salad, or shopped efficiently and only have to walk to your fridge, remember that the most important things about cooking at home are as follows: have fun, cook well, and eat great food!

20 Minutes or LESS

SIMPLE ITALIAN WEDDING SOUP

Prep time: 10 minutes **Cook time:** 1 minute **Total:** 11 minutes

This simple classic soup is a no-brainer for this quick and easy cookbook. Feel free to use either chicken or beef stock or a combination of the two—whatever you prefer will work here. Kind of an Italian version of egg drop soup, if you will.

6 cups chicken stock, or canned, low-sodium chicken broth

2 cups beef stock or canned, low-sodium beef broth

4 large eggs, beaten

¼ cup plus 2 tablespoons finely grated Parmigiano-Reggiano cheese

¼ cup plus 2 tablespoons finely chopped mixed fresh herbs (such as parsley, marjoram, and basil)

Pinch of ground nutmeg

Salt and freshly ground black pepper

1. Pour the stock into a 3-quart saucepan and bring to a simmer.

2. While you are waiting for the stock to simmer, prep the rest of the ingredients. Combine the eggs, Parmesan, herbs, and nutmeg in a medium mixing bowl and whisk to combine.

3. When the stock is simmering, use a large fork to drizzle in the egg mixture while continuously stirring the stock. Continue to simmer until the egg is just set, about 45 seconds. Remove from the heat and season with salt and pepper to taste. Serve immediately.

4 to 6 servings

SWEET PEA SOUP

Prep time: 7 minutes **Cook time:** 9 minutes **Total:** 16 minutes

This soup is sublime—in method, in timing, in appearance, and in taste. Sweet peas are simmered in a flavorful broth and pureed with fresh spinach. Dollop with the lemony sour cream. Enjoy sir, enjoy madam.

1/2 cup sour cream

1 teaspoon freshly squeezed lemon juice

1/2 teaspoon lemon zest

2 tablespoons butter

1 1/4 cups thinly sliced onion (about 1 medium onion)

1 medium clove garlic, thinly sliced

3 sprigs fresh mint

3 sprigs fresh parsley

4 cups vegetable stock or canned, low-sodium vegetable broth

1 pound frozen green peas

1/2 teaspoon salt

1/4 teaspoon freshly ground white pepper

1 1/2 cups packed prewashed spinach (about 2 ounces)

1. Combine the sour cream, lemon juice, and lemon zest. Cover and refrigerate until ready to use.

2. Melt the butter in a 4-quart or larger pot over medium-high heat. Add the onion and garlic and cook until soft and translucent, 4 minutes.

3. Gather the herbs into a bunch and secure with kitchen twine. Add the vegetable stock and the herb bundle to the onion, cover, and bring to a boil. Uncover, reduce the heat to a simmer, and cook for 3 minutes. Increase the heat to high, return the soup to a boil, and add the peas. Bring the soup back to a boil, reduce the heat, and simmer for 2 minutes longer. Remove the soup from the heat. Remove the herb bundle. Stir in the salt, white pepper, and spinach.

4. Puree the soup using an immersion blender or in two batches using a blender (see Note). Serve immediately with a dollop of the lemony sour cream.

Note: Please use caution when blending hot liquids; blend only small amounts at a time, with the blender tightly covered and a kitchen towel held over the top.

About 1 1/2 quarts, 4 to 6 servings

SHRIMP AND CHORIZO TAPAS

Prep time: 7 minutes **Cook time:** 13 minutes **Total:** 20 minutes

Impress your guests with this unique combination of spicy chorizo and sweet shrimp . . . so simple and tasty! The trick is to use the best chorizo sausage you can find, the freshest shrimp available, and a good-quality olive oil.

1 tablespoon plus $1/4$ cup Spanish olive oil

1 pound firm (smoked) chorizo, cut on the diagonal into $1/2$-inch-thick slices

$1^{1}/_{2}$ cups thinly sliced onions

1 tablespoon minced garlic

$1/2$ cup dry (fino) sherry

$1^{1}/_{2}$ pounds medium shrimp, peeled and deveined

1 tablespoon Spanish paprika

1 teaspoon salt

$1/2$ teaspoon freshly ground black pepper

3 tablespoons freshly squeezed lemon juice

2 tablespoons minced fresh parsley

Crusty bread, for serving

1. Place a large skillet over medium-high heat, and add the 1 tablespoon olive oil. When it is hot, add the sliced chorizo and sauté, turning as necessary, until it begins to brown around the edges on both sides, 4 to 6 minutes. Add the onions and cook, stirring occasionally, until caramelized around the edges and softened, 4 to 6 minutes. Add the garlic and cook, stirring, for 30 seconds. Add $1/4$ cup of the sherry and cook for 1 minute.

2. Add the shrimp, paprika, salt, and pepper and cook, stirring occasionally, until the shrimp are pink and just cooked through, about 4 minutes. Add the remaining $1/4$ cup sherry, the remaining $1/4$ cup olive oil, and the lemon juice and parsley; stir to combine. When heated through, remove from the heat.

3. Serve immediately on small plates, with any accumulated cooking juices spooned over the top. Pass the bread at the table.

6 to 8 servings

HERBED OLIVES

Prep time: 8 minutes **Total:** 8 minutes

If you buy olives that are already marinated, make them special by adding the fennel, thyme, rosemary, and orange peel. Or marinate plain olives as outlined below. A perfect starter or snack any time of the day!

1 pound assorted olives, such as Kalamata, Cerignola, Greek, Gaeta, and/or Niçoise, drained

1½ cups olive oil

1 onion, julienned (see Note)

4 cloves garlic, thinly sliced

4 bay leaves, torn into pieces

1 teaspoon fennel seeds

2 sprigs fresh thyme

1 sprig fresh rosemary

3-inch-long strip of orange peel, julienned

12 coriander seeds

¼ teaspoon crushed red pepper, or to taste

1. Combine all the ingredients in a large bowl, and stir well. Serve immediately, or marinate overnight before serving.

2. Transfer any leftovers to glass jars with lids, and refrigerate for up to 2 weeks. (Allow to return to room temperature before serving.)

Notes: Don't discard the remaining olive oil after the olives are gone—it is delicious served as a dipping oil for crusty French bread or drizzled over pasta or grilled vegetables.

"Julienned" means cut into thin strips about the size of matchsticks.

About 1 quart

ROASTED RED PEPPER HUMMUS

Prep time: 18 minutes **Total:** 18 minutes

I absolutely love hummus, and what a spin on the classic—adding roasted red peppers, crushed red pepper, and cumin. We suggest serving this with bread or chips, but it also works well as a dip with crudités or even as a spread for sandwiches!

Two 15-ounce cans chickpeas, drained

¾ cup (about 6 ounces) jarred roasted red peppers, drained and coarsely chopped

3 large cloves garlic

1½ teaspoons salt, plus more to taste

½ teaspoon crushed red pepper

½ cup tahini

½ cup water

4 to 6 tablespoons freshly squeezed lemon juice, plus more for drizzling

4 to 6 tablespoons olive oil, plus more for drizzling

⅛ teaspoon cayenne pepper

⅛ teaspoon ground cumin

1 teaspoon chopped fresh parsley

¼ teaspoon sweet paprika

Pita bread or pita chips, for serving

1. Place the chickpeas and chopped roasted red pepper in the bowl of a food processor.

2. On a cutting board, use the side of a knife to mash the garlic cloves with ¼ teaspoon of the salt, forming a smooth paste. Add this to the processor along with the crushed red pepper, tahini, water, 4 tablespoons of the lemon juice, 4 tablespoons of the olive oil, the remaining 1¼ teaspoons salt, cayenne, and cumin. Process until smooth, stopping to scrape down the sides of the bowl as needed. Taste, and adjust the seasoning by adding more salt, lemon juice, and / or olive oil as needed.

3. Transfer the hummus to a wide, shallow bowl for serving. Drizzle with lemon juice and olive oil, and sprinkle with the parsley and paprika. Serve with pita bread wedges or chips.

Note: If you prefer a traditional plain hummus, simply omit the roasted red peppers and decrease the garlic to 2 cloves.

3 cups

BALSAMIC-MARINATED CREMINI MUSHROOMS

Prep time: 18 minutes **Total:** 18 minutes

Did you know that cremini mushrooms are the little baby siblings of the portobello mushroom? The addition of Italian herbs and grated pecorino makes this really yummy.

. . . .

1/4 cup balsamic vinegar

2 teaspoons minced garlic

1 1/2 teaspoons dried Italian herbs, crushed with your fingers

1 teaspoon salt

1/4 teaspoon freshly ground black pepper

3/4 cup extra-virgin olive oil

2 pounds cremini mushrooms, wiped clean, stemmed, and quartered

1/4 cup finely grated Pecorino Romano cheese

1. In a small bowl, whisk together the balsamic vinegar, garlic, Italian herbs, salt, and pepper. Gradually add the olive oil, whisking constantly.

2. In a large bowl, combine the mushrooms and marinade, and toss to coat evenly. Cover and refrigerate until ready to serve, up to 24 hours.

3. Return to room temperature before serving, and garnish with the cheese. Serve with toothpicks or on small plates with forks.

About 1 quart

BRUSCHETTA

Prep time: 12 minutes Cook time: 4 minutes Total: 16 minutes

A simple Italian delight: slices of crusty bread topped with diced fresh tomatoes that have been tossed with olive oil, herbs, garlic, and salt. Wait until the tomatoes are in their peak season for the best flavor. Try this as a starter to any quick meal. Be sure to use a timer when toasting the bread slices—these toast really fast!

1 pound medium-ripe tomatoes, cored and cut into $1/2$-inch dice

$1/2$ cup thinly sliced fresh basil

$3/4$ teaspoon fine sea salt

$1/2$ teaspoon freshly ground black pepper

6 tablespoons extra-virgin olive oil

1 teaspoon minced garlic

Thirty $1/2$-inch-thick slices Italian or French bread (as crusty as you can find)

1. Position a rack as close as possible to the broiler element and preheat the broiler.

2. In a small serving bowl, combine the tomatoes, basil, sea salt, pepper, and 3 tablespoons of the olive oil. Set aside.

3. In another small bowl, combine the garlic and the remaining 3 tablespoons olive oil.

4. Lay the slices of bread on a baking sheet. Broil on both sides until golden and crispy, about $1\frac{1}{2}$ minutes per side. Remove from the oven and brush the tops of the slices with the garlic oil. Return the baking sheet to the broiler for 30 seconds. Transfer the toast slices to a large platter and serve immediately, with the tomato mixture alongside for guests to spoon over the toasts.

6 to 8 servings

MOZZARELLA AND TOMATO BITES WITH KALAMATA OLIVE DRIZZLE

Prep time: 20 minutes **Total:** 20 minutes

This dish makes a gorgeous presentation: the contrasting colors of the bright red cherry tomatoes, green basil, and white mozzarella skewered together will make your guests feel that you put in a lot of effort to impress them (but it's pretty easy to put together, and I won't tell if you don't). Drizzle the olive mixture on top and, oh, baby, your guests will be screaming for the next course!

20 to 25 small grape or cherry tomatoes, halved

40 to 50 small fresh basil leaves

8 ounces ciliegine (see Note), drained and patted dry, halved

1/4 cup chopped pitted Kalamata olives

1/2 cup extra-virgin olive oil

1/4 teaspoon minced garlic

1/4 teaspoon crushed red pepper

2 tablespoons minced fresh oregano or marjoram

1/4 teaspoon salt

Kosher salt, for garnish

1. Using small decorative cocktail skewers or bamboo toothpicks, skewer 1 tomato half, 1 basil leaf, and 1 ciliegine half onto each skewer, kebab-fashion, with the basil leaf sandwiched between the mozzarella and tomato halves and the cut sides of the tomato and mozzarella facing each other. Repeat until you have used all of the ciliegine halves. You should have about 42 filled skewers. Arrange on a small serving platter and set aside.

2. In the bowl of a blender or food processor, combine the olives, olive oil, garlic, crushed red pepper, oregano, and salt, and process until smooth. Drizzle the olive mixture over the tomato-mozzarella skewers. Sprinkle the entire platter with kosher salt, and serve immediately.

Note: Ciliegine are cherry-size balls of fresh mozzarella, available at upscale Italian markets and some gourmet grocery stores. If these are unavailable in your area, simply substitute 1-inch cubes of fresh mozzarella.

About 42 hors d'oeuvres

EMERIL'S SALAD

Prep time: 8 minutes **Total:** 8 minutes

This is a simplified version of the signature salad served at Emeril's Restaurant in New Orleans. It's been on the menu since day one. Try it and you'll see why folks keep asking for it after all these years.

8 cups (about 4 ounces) loosely packed assorted baby salad greens

1/2 cup (about 3 ounces) grated pepper Jack cheese

1/4 teaspoon chopped fresh rosemary

1/4 teaspoon chopped fresh thyme

1/4 cup (about 2 ounces) whole oil-packed sundried tomatoes, drained and julienned

2 tablespoons balsamic vinegar

2 tablespoons extra-virgin olive oil

Salt and freshly ground black pepper

Simple Croutons (page 136) or store-bought croutons, for serving (optional)

4 tablespoons alfalfa sprouts or broccoli sprouts

1. To assemble the salad, place the greens, cheese, and chopped herbs in a large mixing bowl. Add the julienned sundried tomatoes. Drizzle the balsamic vinegar and extra-virgin olive oil over the salad, and season with salt and pepper to taste. Toss to coat well.

2. Divide the salad equally among four salad plates. Place 4 or 5 croutons on each plate, and top each salad with 1 tablespoon of the sprouts. Serve immediately.

4 servings

REAL CAESAR SALAD

Prep time: 15 minutes **Total:** 15 minutes

I bet you never dreamed that this classic salad could be on your table in less than 20 minutes!

. . . .

1 egg

3 large canned anchovy fillets

2 cloves garlic

2 tablespoons freshly squeezed
   lemon juice

1½ teaspoons whole-grain
   mustard

¾ cup olive oil

¼ cup extra-virgin olive oil

¾ cup (about 2 ounces) grated
   Parmigiano-Reggiano cheese

⅛ teaspoon Tabasco sauce

¼ teaspoon Worcestershire sauce

1 teaspoon salt

1 teaspoon freshly ground black
   pepper

3 romaine hearts (one 12-ounce
   bag), cut into 1-inch pieces,
   rinsed and spun dry

2 cups Simple Croutons (page 136)
   or store-bought croutons

1. Place the egg, anchovies, garlic, lemon juice, and mustard in the bowl of a food processor and process until smooth, about 1 minute. While the machine is running, slowly drizzle in the olive oil and the extra-virgin olive oil until completely incorporated, smooth, and thick.

2. Stop processing and add ¼ cup of the cheese, the Tabasco, the Worcestershire, ¾ teaspoon of the salt, and ¾ teaspoon of the pepper. Pulse to combine.

3. Transfer the Caesar dressing to a small container. (Covered, it will keep in the refrigerator for up to 1 week.)

4. In a large mixing bowl, combine the lettuce, the remaining ½ cup cheese, remaining ¼ teaspoon salt, remaining ¼ teaspoon black pepper, and the croutons. Toss to combine. Add ½ cup plus 2 tablespoons of the dressing, and toss again. Serve immediately.

Note: We advise using caution when consuming raw egg products; children or other individuals with compromised immune systems should take care due to the slight risk of salmonella or other food-borne illness. To reduce this risk, we recommend using only fresh, properly refrigerated, clean grade A or AA eggs with intact shells.

4 servings (1¾ cups dressing)

SPINACH SALAD WITH BACON AND FRIED EGGS

Prep time: 10 minutes Cook time: 9 minutes Total: 19 minutes

Bacon, eggs, and spinach. Oh, baby. What a classic combination, what a simple way to get dinner on the table in no time.

. . . .

10 ounces thick-sliced bacon, cut into 1/2-inch-wide pieces

1 tablespoon olive oil

4 large eggs

1/4 cup minced shallots

4 tablespoons red wine vinegar

1/2 teaspoon salt, plus more to taste

1/4 teaspoon freshly ground black pepper, plus more to taste

One 10-ounce bag prewashed spinach, any thick stems removed

1. Set a 10-inch sauté pan over medium heat and add the bacon. Cook, stirring often, until most of the fat has been rendered and the bacon is crisp, 7 to 8 minutes.

2. During the last few minutes the bacon is cooking, heat the oil over medium heat in another large non-stick sauté pan. Add the eggs and cook until the white is firm and the yolk is cooked to your liking, about 1 minute for a runny yolk and longer for a firmer yolk. Set the pan aside and keep warm.

3. Use a slotted spoon to transfer the bacon pieces to a paper towel–lined plate. Add the shallots to the pan and sauté until fragrant and soft, about 1 minute. Add the red wine vinegar, salt, and pepper. Stir to combine and then remove from the heat.

4. Place the spinach in a large bowl, and working quickly, add about half of the hot vinaigrette from the pan. Toss carefully.

5. Divide the spinach equally among four serving plates. Arrange an egg on top of each mound of spinach, season with salt and black pepper, and sprinkle with the crisp bacon. Drizzle with additional vinaigrette if desired, and serve immediately.

4 servings

ORANGE, WALNUT, AND GOAT CHEESE SALAD

Prep time: 19 minutes Total: 19 minutes

There is something immensely satisfying about the combination of simple greens, toasted nuts, fresh oranges, and goat cheese. If you like, add thin slices of grilled or broiled chicken breast to this salad for a complete meal.

1/2 cup roughly chopped walnuts

2 medium oranges

8 ounces mesclun salad greens or spring greens mix

2 shallots, cut into thin rings (about 1/3 cup)

5 tablespoons olive oil

2 tablespoons balsamic vinegar

1/4 teaspoon salt, plus more to taste

1/8 teaspoon freshly ground black pepper, plus more to taste

1/8 teaspoon sugar

3 ounces soft, mild goat cheese, crumbled

1. Preheat the oven to 350°F.

2. Spread the walnuts on a small baking sheet and toast until fragrant and lightly colored, 5 to 6 minutes. Set aside until cooled slightly.

3. Cut away the peels from the oranges, leaving no white pith. Holding them over a small bowl, segment the oranges, catching any juices (see page 19).

4. In a large bowl, combine the greens, orange segments, and shallot rings.

5. In a small bowl, combine the oil, vinegar, salt, pepper, sugar, and 2 tablespoons of the reserved orange juice. Whisk to combine. Taste, and adjust the seasoning if necessary. Drizzle the dressing over the salad, tossing to coat it evenly. Add the goat cheese and chopped walnuts, and toss gently to combine. Season lightly with salt and pepper if desired, and serve immediately.

4 to 6 servings

1 Using a sharp knife, cut away the peel from the orange on all sides, leaving the orange completely free of any white pith. Working over a small bowl, segment the orange by cutting in between the membranes on both sides of each segment.

2 Use the edge of the knife to help release the segments into the bowl.

3 Repeat until the orange is completely segmented. Squeeze the membranes over the bowl to release any remaining juices.

CUCUMBER RIBBON SALAD

Prep time: 19 minutes **Total:** 19 minutes

This simple cucumber salad is equally good with or without smoked salmon.

. . . .

3 tablespoons olive oil

3 tablespoons minced shallot

2½ tablespoons freshly squeezed lemon juice

2 tablespoons chopped fresh mint

2 tablespoons chopped fresh dill

½ teaspoon grated lemon zest

1 teaspoon salt

½ teaspoon freshly ground white pepper

1 teaspoon superfine sugar

3 English (seedless) cucumbers, peeled

4 ounces smoked salmon (optional)

1. Whisk together the olive oil, shallot, lemon juice, mint, dill, and lemon zest in a small bowl; season with the salt, white pepper, and sugar.

2. Cut the cucumbers in half crosswise. Using a vegetable peeler, peel long strips to form ribbons, and place the ribbons in a salad bowl. Add the dressing and toss to combine.

3. Arrange the cucumber ribbons on four salad plates. If using, tuck slices of salmon in among the ribbons, or drape them loosely over all. Serve immediately.

4 first-course servings

ANTIPASTO PASTA SALAD

Prep time: 11 minutes **Cook time:** 8 minutes **Total:** 19 minutes

Everyone who knows me knows that I'm a big fan of charcuterie of all sorts—salami, pepperoni, sausages, you name it. Here the most basic salami elevates a simple pasta salad to something more substantial. Save time by buying pre-packaged thinly sliced salami.

2 tablespoons plus $\frac{1}{2}$ teaspoon salt

1 pound fusilli pasta

1 tablespoon minced garlic

$\frac{1}{4}$ cup balsamic vinegar

$\frac{1}{2}$ teaspoon freshly ground black pepper

$\frac{1}{2}$ teaspoon crushed red pepper

$\frac{1}{2}$ cup extra-virgin olive oil

$\frac{1}{2}$ cup plus 2 tablespoons finely grated Pecorino Romano cheese

$\frac{1}{2}$ cup sliced pitted Kalamata olives

$\frac{1}{2}$ cup finely sliced pepperoncini

$\frac{1}{2}$ cup julienned salami slices

2 tablespoons chopped mixed fresh herbs (such as parsley and basil)

1. Combine the 2 tablespoons salt and 4 quarts of water in a large pot and bring to a boil over high heat. Add the pasta and cook, stirring occasionally to keep the pasta from sticking together, until just tender, 6 to 8 minutes.

2. While the pasta is cooking, assemble the remaining ingredients and make the vinaigrette: Using the back of a wooden spoon, make a paste of the garlic and remaining $\frac{1}{2}$ teaspoon salt in a large bowl. Whisk in the balsamic vinegar, black pepper, and crushed red pepper. Gradually whisk in the olive oil.

3. Drain the pasta and rinse it under cold running water. Drain again. Transfer the pasta to a large mixing bowl and add the vinaigrette, along with the cheese, olives, pepperoncini, salami, and herbs. Toss to mix. Serve immediately, or cover and refrigerate until ready to serve (see Note) (let the salad return to room temperature before serving).

Note: If the salad sits for any length of time before you serve it, you may need to drizzle a bit of extra vinegar and olive oil over it and toss to mix.

4 to 6 servings

CANTALOUPE, PROSCIUTTO, AND ARUGULA SALAD

Prep time: 20 minutes **Total:** 20 minutes

This salad should be attempted only when melons are in season—it's a great addition to an al fresco dinner in the heat of summer. So simple, so refreshing, so satisfying. Don't skip the prosciutto—it's what makes this dish. Try using the best-quality prosciutto that you can find, preferably a variety from Italy or Spain. It can be pricey, but a little goes a long way here.

1/4 cup champagne vinegar or white wine vinegar

1 tablespoon minced shallot

1/2 teaspoon minced garlic

1/2 teaspoon Dijon mustard

1/2 teaspoon salt, plus more to taste

1/4 teaspoon freshly ground black pepper, plus more to taste

1/2 cup vegetable oil or vegetable-olive oil blend

1 tablespoon minced mixed fresh herbs (such as basil, chives, and parsley)

8 ounces fresh arugula, rinsed and spun dry

1/2 cup thinly sliced red onion

1 cantaloupe, halved, seeded, peeled, and cut into thin wedges

6 to 8 thin slices prosciutto, torn into bite-size pieces

1. In a mixing bowl, combine the vinegar, shallot, garlic, mustard, salt, and pepper and whisk to combine. While continuously whisking, add the oil in a slow, steady stream until completely incorporated. Whisk in the herbs, and set aside while you prepare the salad.

2. In a large bowl, combine the arugula and red onion. Drizzle in 1/4 cup of the vinaigrette and toss to combine. Add more vinaigrette to taste, if desired, and season lightly with salt and pepper. Toss gently to combine.

3. Arrange the cantaloupe wedges on a large serving plate, top with the arugula salad and the prosciutto. Serve immediately.

Note: Any unused vinaigrette can be stored in a nonreactive, airtight container in the refrigerator for up to 2 days.

4 to 6 servings

ORANGE, FENNEL, AND BLACK OLIVE SALAD

Prep time: 13 minutes **Cook time:** 17 minutes **Total:** 20 minutes (prep and cook times overlap)

This classic Mediterranean flavor combination is hard to beat.

. . . .

2 cups freshly squeezed orange juice

2 medium fennel bulbs (7 ounces each)

1 large red onion (10 ounces)

1¹/₂ cups pitted Kalamata olives, drained

6 large California navel oranges (12 ounces each)

¹/₂ teaspoon grated orange zest

2 tablespoons red wine vinegar

1 tablespoon minced shallot

1 teaspoon honey

¹/₄ cup extra-virgin olive oil, plus more for drizzling (optional)

Salt and freshly ground black pepper

1. Place the orange juice in a small saucepan and bring to a boil. Continue to cook at a simmer until reduced in volume to about ¹/₄ cup, about 17 minutes (be careful near the end of cooking, as this can easily burn if left unattended). Allow the reduced orange juice to cool to room temperature.

2. While the orange juice is reducing, trim off and discard the ends of the fennel bulbs, reserving a few fronds for garnish. Cut the fennel bulbs into thin crosswise slices, and place them in a salad bowl. Cut the onion into thin julienne (see page 7). Pit the olives and cut them in half. Add the onion and olives to the salad bowl.

3. Using a sharp knife, cut away the peels from the oranges, leaving no white pith. Holding them over a small bowl, segment the oranges, cutting in between the membranes to release each segment and letting them fall into the bowl (see page 19). Refrigerate until you are ready to serve the salad.

4. Transfer the cooled reduced orange juice to a mixing bowl, and add the orange zest, red wine vinegar, shallot, and honey. Whisk thoroughly to combine. Add the oil in a thin, steady stream, whisking all the time, until completely incorporated and emulsified. Season with salt and pepper to taste.

5. Arrange the orange segments over the fennel, red onion, and olives, and drizzle with the vinaigrette. Toss gently to combine. Serve the salad garnished with some of the reserved fennel fronds, and drizzled with additional olive oil if desired.

4 servings

ICEBERG WEDGES WITH CHERRY TOMATO VINAIGRETTE

Prep time: 20 minutes **Total:** 20 minutes

Iceberg sometimes gets a bad rap, especially as of late, with the advent of fancy specialty lettuces and microgreens, but sometimes there is nothing like a cool, crisp wedge of iceberg with a tasty dressing. Here I've made it special by serving it with a simple cherry tomato vinaigrette and two of my favorite cheeses.

. . . .

$1/3$ cup sliced shallots

3 tablespoons balsamic vinegar

3 tablespoons red wine vinegar

$3/4$ cup extra-virgin olive oil

1 pint cherry tomatoes, halved

1 tablespoon chopped fresh basil

1 tablespoon chopped fresh parsley

$1 1/4$ teaspoons salt

$1 1/4$ teaspoons freshly ground black pepper

1 large head (about 1 pound) iceberg lettuce, cored and cut into 8 wedges

1 cup (about 4 ounces) grated fresh mozzarella cheese

1 cup (about 4 ounces) grated or crumbled blue cheese

1. In a medium bowl, combine the shallots, balsamic vinegar, and red wine vinegar. While stirring with a spoon, drizzle in the extra-virgin olive oil. Add the tomatoes, basil, parsley, 1 teaspoon of the salt, and 1 teaspoon of the pepper. Mix well to combine, and set aside.

2. Arrange 2 wedges of iceberg against each other on each of four serving plates. Season the iceberg with the remaining $1/4$ teaspoon salt and $1/4$ teaspoon black pepper. Sprinkle $1/4$ cup mozzarella and $1/4$ cup blue cheese over each plate. Then generously spoon the tomato vinaigrette over all, dividing it evenly among the salads.

4 servings

SALAD TROPICALE

Prep time: 20 minutes **Total:** 20 minutes

Here we have a composed salad. Instead of tossing everything together, the ingredients are arranged over the lettuce in neat, separate piles for an interesting display. This salad takes its name from the combination of hearts of palm, tomatoes, and avocados. These three tropical ingredients, combined with just about any dressing you like, make for a refreshing salad that just screams, "Take me to the islands!"

1 large head Bibb lettuce

1/4 teaspoon salt

1/4 teaspoon freshly ground black pepper

One 14-ounce jar hearts of palm, drained and cut diagonally into quarters

2 medium-size vine-ripened tomatoes, each cut into 8 wedges

2 firm-ripe Hass avocados, halved, seeded, and sliced

1 cucumber, halved lengthwise and cut into 1/4-inch-thick half-moons

3/4 cup Herb Vinaigrette or Buttermilk Dressing (pages 32, 29)

1. Halve and core the Bibb lettuce. Gently separate the leaves; rinse and spin dry. Divide the lettuce among four plates, arranging the leaves so as to create a bowl on each plate. Sprinkle the lettuce bowls with the salt and pepper.

2. Divide the heart of palm pieces, tomatoes, avocados, and cucumbers evenly among the four plates, forming neat individual piles of each within the lettuce bowls. Spoon 3 generous tablespoons of vinaigrette or dressing over each salad. Serve immediately.

4 servings

BUTTERMILK DRESSING

Prep time: 10 minutes **Total:** 10 minutes

This creamy dressing just needs to be stirred together and that's it. Kick it up by adding minced herbs to your liking, or add up to ¾ cup crumbled blue cheese to the basic recipe for a rich and creamy blue cheese dressing. Perfect for a crisp wedge of iceberg lettuce!

5 tablespoons buttermilk

¼ cup mayonnaise

¼ cup sour cream

1 tablespoon freshly squeezed lemon juice

2 tablespoons minced green onion tops

1 teaspoon minced garlic

¼ teaspoon finely grated lemon zest

¼ teaspoon salt

¼ teaspoon freshly ground white pepper

¼ teaspoon Emeril's Original Essence or Creole Seasoning

Whisk all the ingredients together in a nonreactive mixing bowl. Use immediately, or store in a covered nonreactive container in the refrigerator for up to 3 days.

1 cup

Creole Seasoning

2½ tablespoons paprika
2 tablespoons salt
2 tablespoons garlic powder
1 tablespoon black pepper
1 tablespoon onion powder
1 tablespoon cayenne pepper
1 tablespoon dried oregano
1 tablespoon dried thyme

Combine all the ingredients thoroughly.

⅔ cup

BALSAMIC VINAIGRETTE

Prep time: 8 minutes **Total:** 8 minutes

A simple vinaigrette that is equally at home on mixed greens, grilled veggies or chicken, or pasta salads.

. . . .

5 tablespoons balsamic vinegar

1 teaspoon Dijon mustard

1 teaspoon sugar

$1/2$ teaspoon salt

$1/4$ teaspoon freshly ground black pepper

1 clove garlic, smashed

5 tablespoons extra-virgin olive oil

5 tablespoons olive oil

In a nonreactive mixing bowl, whisk together the vinegar, mustard, sugar, salt, pepper, and garlic. While whisking, add the oils in a thin, steady stream until they are completely incorporated and the dressing is emulsified. Use immediately, or refrigerate in a covered nonreactive container for up to 1 week.

This is best if allowed to sit for at least 10 minutes to allow the garlic to infuse. (Discard the garlic before serving.)

About 1 cup

RED WINE VINAIGRETTE

Prep time: 10 minutes **Total:** 10 minutes

This is a classic French-style vinaigrette. Serve it over mixed greens, poached leeks or asparagus, grilled chicken, or even poached fish.

. . . .

1/4 cup red wine vinegar

2 tablespoons minced shallot

1 1/2 teaspoons Dijon mustard

3/4 teaspoon salt

1/4 teaspoon freshly ground black pepper

3/4 cup canola or vegetable oil

In a medium bowl, whisk together the vinegar, shallot, mustard, salt, and pepper. While constantly whisking, add the oil in a thin, steady stream until it is completely incorporated and the vinaigrette is emulsified. Serve immediately, or refrigerate in a covered nonreactive container for up to 2 days.

1 generous cup

HERB VINAIGRETTE

Prep time: 18 minutes **Total:** 18 minutes

Use whichever herbs you like, or whichever you have on hand, to make this simple vinaigrette.

. . . .

¼ cup white wine vinegar

1 tablespoon minced shallot

1 tablespoon Dijon mustard

½ teaspoon salt, plus more to taste

¼ teaspoon freshly ground black pepper, plus more to taste

½ cup vegetable oil (such as canola)

2 tablespoons extra-virgin olive oil

4 tablespoons chopped mixed fresh soft herbs (such as parsley, chives, basil, and tarragon)

In a medium bowl, whisk together the vinegar, shallot, mustard, salt, and pepper. While constantly whisking, add the oils in a thin, steady stream until they are completely incorporated and the dressing is emulsified. Stir in the herbs, and adjust the seasoning to taste if necessary. Serve immediately or refrigerate in a covered nonreactive container for up to 2 days.

1 generous cup

SAUSAGE AND PEPPER PO-BOY

Prep time: 8 minutes **Cook time:** 10 to 12 minutes **Total:** 18 to 20 minutes

This is my rendition of the traditional Italian sandwich, which is also popular at New York City's street festivals—it is a favorite at the San Gennaro festival in Little Italy. I have added a New Orleans spin here by kicking the mayo up with a little Louisiana hot sauce.

2 tablespoons olive oil

1 red bell pepper, thinly sliced

1 green bell pepper, thinly sliced

2 cups sliced yellow onions

2 teaspoons Emeril's Original Essence or Creole Seasoning (page 29)

1 teaspoon dried Italian herbs

1 pound mild Italian sausage, removed from casings and crumbled

1/2 cup mayonnaise

1 tablespoon Louisiana hot sauce or other red hot sauce

1 loaf soft French bread, cut into four 6-inch sections, each section sliced in half horizontally

4 ounces sliced provolone cheese

1. In a large sauté pan, heat the olive oil over medium-high heat. When the oil is hot, add the bell peppers, onions, Essence, and Italian herbs. Cook until the vegetables have softened, 4 to 5 minutes. Transfer the peppers and onions to a paper towel–lined plate.

2. Add the crumbled sausage to the hot pan and cook until the meat is cooked through and lightly browned, about 5 minutes. Set aside.

3. Preheat the broiler.

4. In a small bowl, combine the mayonnaise and the hot sauce.

5. To assemble the po-boys, spread the cut sides of each piece of bread with the spicy mayonnaise. Divide the sausage evenly among the 4 bottom pieces of bread, then top evenly with the peppers and onions. Arrange the cheese slices over the filled bottom halves and over the cut side of each top portion (cut the cheese to fit as necessary).

6. Place the sandwich halves on a baking sheet, cheese sides up, and heat under the broiler just until the cheese melts, 1 to 2 minutes. Press the sandwich halves together, and serve immediately.

4 servings

BACON, LETTUCE, AVOCADO, AND TOMATO SANDWICH WITH BASIL MAYO

Prep time: 10 minutes **Cook time:** 10 minutes **Total:** 20 minutes

The addition of creamy avocado slices takes this simple classic up a notch and makes it even more delicious and satisfying. And the basil mayo, well, now, what's not to love?

16 slices thick-cut bacon

8 slices (about $\frac{1}{2}$ inch thick) brioche, challah, or other soft white bread

$\frac{1}{2}$ cup mayonnaise

2 packed tablespoons finely chopped fresh basil

8 to 12 thin slices ripe tomato

8 red-leaf lettuce leaves, rinsed and patted dry

1 ripe avocado, halved, seeded, and sliced

1. Place the bacon in a large skillet or sauté pan over medium heat, and cook until crisp, 6 to 8 minutes. Drain on paper towels while you prepare the remaining ingredients.

2. Toast the bread slices in a toaster to the desired color.

3. Combine the mayonnaise and basil in a small bowl, and stir to mix well.

4. Spread the mayo evenly over one side of each bread slice. Cut or break the bacon slices in half, and arrange on one half of each sandwich. Place 2 or 3 slices of tomato, 2 lettuce leaves, and about one-quarter of the avocado slices on top of the bacon on each sandwich. Top with the other half of the bread, cut the sandwiches in half, and serve immediately.

4 servings

STEAK AND CHEESE SANDWICHES

Prep time: 7 minutes **Cook time:** 13 minutes **Total:** 20 minutes

Steak and tangy blue cheese—ooohhh, how could you go wrong? So fast and yet so good—we could make Philly jealous.

. . . .

1 baguette or other crusty country
    bread, about 24 inches long

6 tablespoons butter:
    4 tablespoons melted,
    2 tablespoons at room
    temperature

2 tablespoons olive oil

4 cups thinly sliced onions

3/4 teaspoon salt

1/2 teaspoon freshly ground black
    pepper

1 pound top sirloin steak

1/4 cup Worcestershire sauce

1/2 cup (about 4 ounces) grated or
    crumbled blue cheese

1. Preheat the oven to 400°F.

2. Cut the baguette into four 6-inch lengths. Split each piece in half horizontally, and brush the insides with the melted butter. Lay the bread, cut side up, on a baking sheet and toast in the oven until crispy, about 10 minutes. Set aside.

3. While the bread is toasting, heat the olive oil in a 14-inch skillet over medium-high heat. Add the onions, 1/2 teaspoon of the salt, and 1/4 teaspoon of the pepper. Cook, stirring as needed, until the onions are nicely browned, about 10 minutes.

4. While the onions are cooking, slice the steak with a very sharp knife into 1/8-inch-thick slices (see Note). Season the steak with the remaining 1/4 teaspoon salt and 1/4 teaspoon pepper.

5. Increase the heat under the skillet to high, move the onions to one side of the pan, and add the softened butter. When it has melted, add the steak and cook for 2 minutes without stirring. Add the Worcestershire and 1/4 cup of the blue cheese. Using tongs or a metal spatula, mix the onions, meat, and cheese together and cook for 1 minute longer. Remove from the heat.

6. Divide the steak mixture, and any accumulated pan juices, evenly among the 4 bottom portions of the toasted bread. Sprinkle with the remaining 1/4 cup cheese, and cover with the toasted bread tops. Serve immediately.

Note: You may find the steak easier to slice thinly if you place it in the freezer for 10 to 15 minutes before slicing.

4 servings

PRESSED ROAST TURKEY, PESTO, AND PROVOLONE SANDWICHES

Prep time: 5 minutes **Cook time:** 12 to 15 minutes **Total:** 17 to 20 minutes

Talk about a delicious quick lunch: slices of turkey and provolone cheese sandwiched with an herbaceous pesto—yum! Try serving these with the Cream of Tomato Soup on page 127 for a true power meal.

. . . .

8 slices ciabatta or other crusty Italian or hearty white sandwich bread

4 tablespoons prepared basil pesto

4 slices (about 4 ounces) provolone cheese

8 slices (about 8 ounces) roast turkey

1½ tablespoons extra-virgin olive oil

1. Lay the bread slices on a clean work surface, and spread 1½ teaspoons of the pesto over one side of each slice of bread. Divide the cheese evenly among the slices (depending on the size of your cheese slices, you may need to cut them in half so that you can have cheese on both sides). Divide the roast turkey slices evenly among 4 of the bread slices. Place the remaining cheese-topped slices on top of the turkey-topped slices to form 4 sandwiches. Brush the outside of each sandwich with some of the olive oil.

2. Preheat a grill pan over medium heat. When it is hot, add the sandwiches, in batches if necessary, and weight them with a sandwich press or another skillet (or other heavy object). Cook until the sandwiches are golden brown and crisp and the cheese has melted, 4 to 6 minutes per side. Remove the sandwiches, cut in half on the diagonal, and serve immediately.

Note: Though we prefer the crisp, ridged exterior you get when these sandwiches are cooked in a grill pan, they can also be cooked in a sauté pan or panini press; the cook time will vary slightly.

4 servings

PROSCIUTTO AND MOZZARELLA PANINI

Prep time: 8 minutes **Cook time:** 8 minutes **Total:** 16 minutes

This is a classic Italian panini. The texture of true Italian ciabatta really makes this sandwich special because it grills up so nice and crisp on the outside.

. . . .

1/4 cup extra-virgin olive oil

1 tablespoon balsamic vinegar

2 teaspoons minced fresh oregano, or 1 teaspoon dried

1 teaspoon minced garlic

1/2 teaspoon salt

1/4 teaspoon freshly ground black pepper

Eight 1/2-inch-thick slices ciabatta or other rustic Italian white bread

4 ounces thinly sliced mozzarella cheese

4 ounces thinly sliced prosciutto

6 ounces jarred roasted red peppers, drained, and torn into 1-inch-wide pieces

1. Whisk the olive oil, vinegar, oregano, garlic, salt, and pepper together in a small bowl to blend.

2. Arrange the slices of bread on a flat work surface, and using a brush, spread the vinaigrette evenly over one side of each slice. Divide the mozzarella equally among the bread slices. Top 4 of the bread slices with the prosciutto and red peppers, and then place the remaining 4 slices of bread on the top, vinaigrette side down, to form 4 sandwiches.

3. Heat a large skillet or grill pan over medium heat. Add the sandwiches and cook, pressing them occasionally with a large spatula or the bottom of a small heavy saucepan, until the bread is golden brown and the cheese has melted, about 4 minutes per side. Serve immediately.

4 servings

OPEN-FACE TURKEY AND CHEESE SANDWICH

Prep time: 12 minutes **Cook time:** 7 minutes **Total:** 19 minutes

This unique combination of flavors is a true showstopper. Trust me on this one—and enjoy!

. . . .

6 ounces soft, mild goat cheese

1 tablespoon finely chopped fresh parsley

1½ teaspoons minced garlic

¼ teaspoon grated lemon zest

1 tablespoon olive oil

8 ounces button mushrooms, wiped clean and sliced

½ teaspoon salt

5 ounces prewashed spinach, any thick stems removed

4½-inch-thick slices hearty white bread (such as sourdough), toasted

¼ cup chopped walnuts, toasted

8 thin slices tomato

8 to 10 ounces sliced roasted turkey breast

4 ounces sliced Emmenthaler or provolone cheese

1. Combine the goat cheese, parsley, ½ teaspoon of the garlic, and the lemon zest in a small bowl and mix well. Set aside.

2. Heat the olive oil in a large nonstick sauté pan over medium-high heat. When it is hot, add the mushrooms and ¼ teaspoon of the salt, and cook, stirring occasionally, until they are soft and caramelized, about 4 minutes. Move the mushrooms aside and add the spinach and the remaining ¼ teaspoon salt to the pan. Stir with the mushrooms and cook until the spinach has almost completely wilted, about 1 minute. Stir in the remaining 1 teaspoon garlic and cook for another 30 seconds. Remove the mushrooms and spinach from the pan and drain off any excess liquid. Set aside until ready to use.

3. Position a rack close to the broiler element and preheat the broiler.

4. Spread the goat cheese mixture evenly over the slices of toasted bread. Sprinkle the walnuts on top. Add 2 slices of tomato on each sandwich, and divide the turkey evenly among the sandwiches, arranging it over the tomatoes. Divide the mushroom-spinach mixture among the sandwiches, then top with the cheese.

5. Place the sandwiches on a baking sheet and broil until the cheese is melted and bubbly, about 1 minute. Serve hot.

4 servings

KICKED-UP TUNA MELTS

Prep time: 15 minutes Cook time: 4 to 5 minutes Total: 19 to 20 minutes

At our house, tuna melts were always on the menu when I was growing up. Add the cheese and just the right amount of heat (whether you griddle it or do a quick broil), and you've got comfort served on a plate. This is a classic!

Four 5-ounce cans solid white tuna packed in water, drained

¼ cup plus 1 tablespoon mayonnaise, plus more for spreading

¼ cup finely chopped red onion

1 tablespoon plus 1 teaspoon nonpareil capers, drained

1 tablespoon freshly squeezed lemon juice

1 teaspoon freshly ground black pepper

½ teaspoon salt

¼ teaspoon dried oregano, crumbled between your fingers

4 slices rustic white bread or other dense white bread

8 thin slices tomato

4 ounces sliced provolone cheese

1. Position a rack about 6 inches from the broiler element and preheat the broiler.

2. Combine the tuna, mayonnaise, red onion, capers, lemon juice, pepper, salt, and oregano in a medium bowl and stir until thoroughly combined.

3. Arrange the bread slices on a baking sheet and spread additional mayonnaise over each slice. Divide the tuna salad evenly among the bread slices, then top with the tomato slices. Arrange the sliced provolone evenly over the sandwiches. Place the baking sheet under the broiler and cook until the cheese is golden and bubbly, 3 to 4 minutes. Serve hot.

4 open-face sandwiches, 2 to 4 servings

FISH TACOS WITH BLACK BEAN SALSA

Prep time: 10 minutes **Cook time:** 10 minutes **Total:** 20 minutes

Use any kind of fresh fish you like for these tacos. (Keep in mind when buying fish that a truly fresh fish should smell like the sea.) Here chunks of the lightly crusted fish combine with the flavors of lime juice, garlic, and black beans, making for a very delicious taco. Kid-friendly, for sure, but also sure to win over any adult.

One 15-ounce can black beans, rinsed and drained

¾ cup olive oil

1 jalapeño, minced (and seeded, if you prefer, for a milder salsa)

1 tablespoon freshly squeezed lime juice

1 teaspoon minced garlic

1½ teaspoons salt

2 pounds skinless firm white fish fillets (such as snapper), trimmed and cut into 3-inch pieces

½ teaspoon freshly ground black pepper

½ cup cornmeal

Eight 6-inch flour tortillas

3 cups thinly sliced or shredded romaine lettuce

4 lime wedges

½ cup sour cream

1. In a medium bowl, combine the black beans, ¼ cup of the olive oil, and the jalapeño, lime juice, garlic, and ½ teaspoon of the salt. Set aside.

2. Season the fish fillets evenly with the remaining 1 teaspoon salt and the black pepper. Dredge quickly in the cornmeal, shaking to remove any excess, and set aside.

3. Heat a 12-inch sauté pan over high heat. Toast each of the tortillas for 30 seconds on one side in the hot sauté pan. Transfer to a plate and cover loosely with a clean kitchen towel to keep warm.

4. In the same sauté pan, heat the remaining ½ cup olive oil over medium-high heat. Add half of the fish fillets, and sauté until just cooked through, about 2 minutes per side. Transfer them to paper towels to drain. Repeat with the remaining fillets.

5. To assemble the tacos, place 2 tortillas on each plate, and divide the shredded lettuce among them. Spoon the black bean mixture onto the lettuce, and divide the fish fillets among the tortillas. Squeeze the lime wedges over the fish, dollop with the sour cream, and fold the tortillas to close. Serve immediately.

4 to 6 servings

FETTUCCINE WITH PEAS AND HAM

Prep time: 8 minutes **Cook time:** 12 minutes **Total:** 20 minutes

Vegetable group? Check. Meat group? Check. Grain group? Check. Dairy group? Check. This dish has it all, making it a great one-dish meal. Serve it with a nice green salad and some hot crusty bread. One of my all-time favorites.

. . . .

$\frac{1}{2}$ teaspoon salt, plus more for the pasta water

1 pound fettuccine

2 teaspoons olive oil

1 cup diced onion

$\frac{1}{4}$ cup thinly sliced shallot

1 tablespoon Emeril's Original Essence or Creole Seasoning (page 29)

1 teaspoon minced garlic

8 ounces ham steak, diced (about 2 cups)

1 cup frozen green peas

2 cups heavy cream

$\frac{1}{4}$ cup chopped fresh parsley

$\frac{1}{2}$ cup grated Parmigiano-Reggiano cheese, plus more for serving (optional)

Freshly ground black pepper, for serving (optional)

1. Bring a large pot of salted water to a boil and cook the fettuccine until al dente, about 12 minutes.

2. While the pasta is cooking, make the sauce: In a 12-inch (or larger) sauté pan, heat the olive oil over medium-high heat. Add the onion, shallot, Essence, and the $\frac{1}{2}$ teaspoon salt, and cook until the onions are translucent, about 2 minutes. Add the garlic, ham, and peas and cook for 2 minutes longer. Increase the heat to high, add the cream, and bring it to a boil. Then reduce the heat to medium and simmer until the cream thickens, about 5 minutes.

3. Drain the pasta in a colander, reserving 1 cup of the cooking water.

4. Add the drained pasta, $\frac{1}{2}$ cup of the reserved cooking water, and the parsley and cheese to the sauce and cook, tossing constantly, until heated through and well combined, about 1 minute. If the mixture seems dry, add the remaining cooking water, a little at a time, as needed.

5. Remove the pan from the heat and transfer the pasta mixture to a large serving bowl or to individual bowls. Sprinkle with additional cheese and black pepper if desired.

4 to 6 servings

(1) Beginning the sauce.

(2) Adding the pasta.

(3) Putting it all together.

ORANGE, CURRANT, AND PINE NUT COUSCOUS

Prep time: 12 minutes **Cook time:** 3 minutes **Inactive time:** 5 minutes **Total:** 20 minutes

This simple couscous side dish is a nice complement to many entrées—and it's pretty, too. The bright flavors of the orange segments and currants create bites of contrasting tastes, and the toasted pine nuts add a bit of texture.

2 cups water

2 tablespoons extra-virgin olive oil

1/2 cup diced red onion or shallots (small dice)

1/2 cup diced carrots (small dice)

1/2 cup dried currants

1 teaspoon grated orange zest

3/4 teaspoon salt

1/2 teaspoon freshly ground white pepper

One 10-ounce package couscous

1 orange, peeled and segmented (see page 19)

1/4 cup pine nuts or chopped walnuts, lightly toasted

1 tablespoon chopped fresh mint or parsley

1. Combine the water, olive oil, red onion, carrots, currants, orange zest, salt, and white pepper in a small saucepan, and bring to a boil. Cook at a slow simmer for 2 minutes to make a flavorful broth.

2. Meanwhile, place the couscous in a medium heat-proof bowl.

3. Pour the hot broth over the couscous and cover with plastic wrap. Allow to steam for 5 minutes.

4. Remove the plastic wrap. Add the orange segments, pine nuts, and mint, and fluff the couscous with a fork. Serve hot.

About 4 cups, 4 servings

LINGUINE ALLA CARBONARA

Prep time: 6 minutes **Cook time:** 12 to 14 minutes **Total:** 18 to 20 minutes

This dish takes its inspiration from many wonderful meals at my friend Mario Batali's restaurant, OTTO, in New York City. Try my quick and easy take on it—my kids go crazy for this dish.

Salt

1 pound linguine

1/4 cup extra-virgin olive oil

1 tablespoon unsalted butter

6 ounces bacon, cut into
 1/2-inch-wide pieces

1 yellow onion (6 ounces), minced

2 teaspoons minced garlic

3 large egg yolks

3/4 cup finely grated Parmigiano-
 Reggiano cheese, at room
 temperature

Freshly ground black pepper, to
 taste

1. Bring a large pot of salted water to a boil, and cook the linguine until al dente, about 9 minutes.

2. While the pasta is cooking, assemble the remaining ingredients and make the sauce: Heat the oil and butter in a large sauté pan over medium heat. Add the bacon and cook until it is beginning to crisp, about 5 minutes. Add the onion and garlic and cook until soft, about 2 minutes. Remove the pan from the heat and set aside.

3. Drain the pasta in a colander, reserving a small amount of the cooking water, and return the pasta to the pot. Place the pot over high heat, add the bacon-onion mixture, and stir until the pasta is coated with the mixture and heated through, 1 minute.

4. Whisk the egg yolks in a small bowl and add them to the pasta, along with the grated cheese. Remove the pot from the heat and toss the pasta until it is well coated. (If needed, add a bit of the reserved cooking water to help toss the pasta.) Season with salt and pepper to taste, and serve immediately.

4 servings

EMERIL'S SHRIMP AND PASTA WITH GARLIC, LEMON, CRUSHED RED PEPPER, AND GREEN ONIONS

Prep time: 8 minutes **Cook time:** 12 minutes **Total:** 20 minutes

The flavors of this dish are all in the title—it's spicy, savory, and bright, and it makes me happy, happy, happy any time of the day. So easy and fast, too!

1 pound linguine

1¼ pounds large shrimp, peeled and deveined

2 teaspoons Emeril's Original Essence or Creole Seasoning (page 29)

8 tablespoons (1 stick) unsalted butter

1 tablespoon minced garlic

½ cup dry white wine

¼ cup freshly squeezed lemon juice

½ teaspoon salt, plus more for the pasta water

⅛ teaspoon freshly ground black pepper

1 teaspoon crushed red pepper

¼ cup chopped green onion tops

2 tablespoons chopped fresh parsley

1. Bring a large pot of salted water to a boil and cook the linguine until al dente, about 9 minutes.

2. While the pasta is cooking, toss the shrimp with the Essence in a medium bowl. Place 4 tablespoons of the butter in a 14-inch skillet set over high heat. Add the shrimp, spreading them evenly in one layer. Cook for 2 minutes, and then turn them to the other side. Add the garlic and cook for 30 seconds. Add the wine, lemon juice, and 2 tablespoons of the remaining butter, and cook for 1½ minutes. Season the shrimp with the ½ teaspoon salt and the black pepper.

3. Drain the pasta in a colander, reserving ½ cup of the cooking water. Add the pasta, reserved cooking water, crushed red pepper, and green onion tops to the sauce in the skillet. Toss until everything is heated through and the pasta is well coated, about 1 minute.

4. Remove the skillet from the heat, add the remaining 2 tablespoons butter and the parsley, and toss to combine. Serve hot.

4 to 6 servings

KICKED-UP SHRIMP FRIED RICE

Prep time: 12 minutes **Cook time:** 6 minutes **Total:** 18 minutes

I love this so much that I usually make extra to eat the day after. Like all stir-fry dishes, it's important that you have all your ingredients prepared and ready to go once you start cooking. Since you must cook this over high heat, take care to constantly toss or stir your ingredients so that nothing gets overcooked. If you don't own a big wok or a skillet that is large enough to do this in one batch, do it in two; just be sure to wipe the pan clean with paper towels in between batches.

4 tablespoons peanut or vegetable oil

3 eggs, lightly beaten

Salt and freshly ground black pepper

8 ounces medium shrimp, peeled and deveined

1/2 teaspoon Emeril's Original Essence or Creole Seasoning (page 29)

3 green onions, white and green parts separately minced

2 teaspoons minced ginger

2 teaspoons minced garlic

3 cups cooked white rice

1 tablespoon dark Asian sesame oil

2 cups (about 12 ounces) frozen stir-fry vegetables, defrosted

2 tablespoons plus 1 teaspoon soy sauce

1. Heat 1 tablespoon of the peanut oil in a large skillet or wok over high heat. When it is hot, add the eggs and a pinch of salt and pepper, and quickly stir until the eggs are fully cooked, moving the skillet off and on the heat as necessary, about 40 seconds. Transfer the eggs to a paper towel–lined plate and set aside. Chop the eggs into small pieces when cool enough to handle.

2. Add 1 tablespoon of the remaining peanut oil to the skillet.

3. In a small bowl, season the shrimp with the Essence and a pinch of salt and pepper. When the oil is hot, add the shrimp to the skillet, in batches if necessary, and cook until pink and lightly caramelized, about 2 minutes per side. Remove from the skillet and set aside.

4. Add the remaining 2 tablespoons peanut oil to the skillet. Add the green onion bottoms (white portion), the ginger, and the garlic, and cook until fragrant, about 15 seconds. Add the rice and cook, tossing, until it is hot and golden, about 2 minutes. Add the sesame oil and the stir-fry vegetables, and cook until heated through, 1 minute. Add the soy sauce, the reserved cooked eggs, and the shrimp, and cook until everything is warmed through, about 1 minute.

5. Season with salt and pepper to taste, garnish with green onion tops, and serve.

4 servings

TURKEY AND WILD RICE SALAD

Prep time: 15 minutes **Total:** 15 minutes

Obviously this is a great choice for the fall season, when leftover holiday turkey is often found lurking in the fridge, but I'm such a fan of roast turkey that I make it year-round.

. . . .

4 cups cooked wild rice mix
   (see Note)

2 cups diced roast turkey breast

1 cup assorted dried fruits (such as cranberry, cherry, and apricot), coarsely chopped

$1/2$ cup coarsely chopped almonds, toasted

Juice and grated zest of 1 orange

$1/4$ cup olive oil

2 tablespoons red wine vinegar

$1/2$ teaspoon salt

$1/4$ teaspoon freshly ground black pepper

Combine all of the ingredients in a large bowl, and toss well to combine. Let stand for 5 minutes, and then serve.

Note: For testing purposes we used a blend of basmati and wild rice, but any cooked rice blend or mix of cooked rices will work here. If the prepared rice has been refrigerated, however, you will need to microwave or steam it briefly to soften it slightly before combining it with the other ingredients.

8 cups, about 8 servings

AROMATIC JASMINE RICE

Prep time: 5 minutes **Cook time:** 15 minutes **Total:** 20 minutes

Bring a taste of Asia into your home with this deliciously nuanced jasmine rice. This dish would be great served alongside Stir-Fried Chicken with Cashews (page 80), Stir-Fried Beef and Broccoli (page 205), or Spicy Pork Stir-Fry with Green Beans (page 95).

2 cups jasmine rice

One 1-inch piece fresh ginger, peeled and halved

Grated zest of 1 lime

1½ cups unsweetened coconut milk

1½ cups chicken broth or canned, low-sodium chicken broth or water

½ teaspoon salt

1 tablespoon chopped fresh cilantro

1 tablespoon crushed peanuts, for garnish

1. Combine all the ingredients except the cilantro and peanuts in a 2-quart saucepan, and stir well to combine. Make sure the aromatics are fully submerged in the rice.

2. Place the pan over high heat and bring the liquid to a boil, stirring occasionally to prevent the rice from sticking to the bottom of the pan. Once it reaches a boil, immediately reduce the heat to low and cover the pan. Cook for 10 minutes. Remove the pan from the heat and allow the rice to steam, covered and undisturbed, for 5 minutes.

3. Discard the ginger. Add the cilantro and gently fluff the rice with a fork. Transfer the rice to a deep serving bowl and garnish with the peanuts. Serve hot or warm.

4 to 6 servings

SPICY SAUSAGE, BEAN, AND CHEESE NACHOS

Prep time: 10 minutes Cook time: 10 minutes Total: 20 minutes

This filling snack is perfect for football season, but don't feel that you have to wait until game time—it's great anytime and can even form the basis of a simple supper when paired with a nice green salad.

1 pound fresh hot sausage (such as chorizo), removed from the casings and crumbled

1/4 cup finely chopped green onion bottoms (reserve tops separately)

1 tablespoon chopped garlic

Two 15-ounce cans pinto or black beans, drained

3/4 cup chicken stock or canned, low-sodium chicken broth or water

1/2 teaspoon chili powder

1/4 teaspoon ground cumin

1/4 teaspoon salt

12 ounces large (restaurant-style) tortilla chips

3 cups grated pepper Jack or sharp cheddar cheese, or a combination

1/4 cup pickled jalapeño slices, or to taste

Your favorite salsa, for serving

Sour cream, for serving

1. Preheat the oven to 450°F.

2. Place a large skillet over medium-high heat, add the sausage, and cook until it is nicely browned and the fat is rendered, about 5 minutes. Use a slotted spoon to transfer the sausage to a paper towel–lined plate to drain.

3. Add the green onion bottoms and the garlic to the fat remaining in the skillet, and cook until fragrant and soft, about 20 seconds. Add the beans, mix well, and cook until heated through, about 1 minute. Add the chicken stock, chili powder, cumin, and salt. Mash the beans with the back of a heavy wooden spoon or a potato masher until chunky-smooth.

4. Reduce the heat to medium and continue cooking until completely warmed through, 1 to 2 minutes. Remove from the heat.

5. Spread half of the tortilla chips in one even layer on a large oval ovenproof platter or in a large baking dish. Top with half of the beans, half of the sausage, half of the cheese, and half of the jalapeños. Repeat with another layer of chips, beans, sausage, cheese, and jalapeños. Bake until the cheese is melted and the mixture is hot, 2 to 3 minutes.

6. Remove from the oven, and serve garnished with chopped green onion tops, salsa, and sour cream.

4 to 6 servings

PAN-ROASTED ASPARAGUS WITH SHIITAKE MUSHROOMS AND CHERRY TOMATOES

Prep time: 8 minutes **Cook time:** 11 to 12 minutes **Total:** 19 to 20 minutes

Asparagus comes in all sizes and can be cooked any number of ways—and to me they are all great—but I especially love asparagus that has been quickly sautéed and then blasted in a very hot oven. In this recipe I have added shiitake mushrooms to give the dish an earthy flavor that strikes a nice balance with the sweetness of the cherry tomatoes.

3 tablespoons olive oil

1 large shallot, sliced crosswise into rings

1 pound asparagus, woody portion of stems removed

4 ounces shiitake mushrooms, wiped clean, stemmed, and quartered

2 ounces cherry or grape tomatoes, quartered

1 teaspoon fresh thyme leaves

1 tablespoon freshly grated Parmigiano-Reggiano cheese

1. Preheat the oven to 400°F.

2. Heat 2 tablespoons of the olive oil in a large oven-proof sauté pan over medium-high heat. When the oil is hot, add the shallot and cook for 30 seconds. Add the asparagus and cook for 3 minutes. Push the asparagus to one side of the pan, and add the remaining 1 tablespoon olive oil and the shiitake mushrooms. Cook for 3 to 4 minutes, allowing the mushrooms to brown. Add the tomatoes and the thyme, and cook for another 2 minutes, tossing the ingredients together.

3. Transfer the pan to the oven and cook for 3 to 4 minutes, or until the asparagus is crisp-tender.

4. Transfer the asparagus mixture to a serving platter, garnish with the cheese, and serve immediately.

**4 side-dish servings or
2 appetizer servings**

GARLICKY BOK CHOY

Prep time: 2 minutes Cook time: 5 to 6 minutes Total: 7 to 8 minutes

If you cannot find baby bok choy in your area, feel free to substitute the same amount of regular bok choy. Regular bok choy will need to be cut into 1½-inch lengths on the diagonal and stirred occasionally while cooking.

2 tablespoons canola oil

1 teaspoon crushed red pepper

1 pound baby bok choy, split in half lengthwise

½ teaspoon salt

2 tablespoons roughly chopped garlic

¼ cup chicken or vegetable stock, or canned, low-sodium chicken or vegetable broth, or water

2 tablespoons butter

Place a 14-inch sauté pan over medium-high heat, and add the oil. When it is hot, add the crushed red pepper and cook until fragrant, about 30 seconds. Add the bok choy, cut sides down, and cook for 1 to 2 minutes. Add the salt, garlic, and chicken stock and cook for 3 minutes, until the stock is mostly reduced. Add the butter to the pan, and when it has melted, turn the bok choy so that it is evenly coated. Remove from the heat and serve immediately.

4 servings

BROILED ZUCCHINI

Prep time: 5 minutes **Cook time:** 15 minutes **Total:** 20 minutes

In this preparation, zucchini is caramelized and roasted with garlic under the broiler—delicious!

2 pounds zucchini

4 cloves garlic

$\frac{1}{4}$ cup olive oil

$1\frac{1}{2}$ teaspoons kosher salt

1 teaspoon freshly ground white pepper

4 sprigs fresh thyme

1. Position a rack 5 or 6 inches from the broiler element and preheat the broiler.

2. Rinse the zucchini and pat it dry. Cut the zucchini in half crosswise; then cut each half lengthwise into 6 to 8 wedges. Smash the garlic cloves, and cut each clove in half.

3. Place the zucchini, garlic, and all the remaining ingredients in a large bowl, and toss well to coat.

4. Place the zucchini mixture in a 12-inch ovenproof skillet, and broil, tossing the pieces occasionally, until it is well caramelized, about 15 minutes.

5. Remove from the broiler, discard the thyme sprigs, and serve immediately.

4 to 6 servings

SAUTÉED YELLOW SQUASH WITH CARROTS AND TARRAGON

Prep time: 12 minutes **Cook time:** 8 minutes **Total:** 20 minutes

This is a beautiful, versatile side dish that can go with just about any entrée. While testing recipes, we enjoyed it with Crispy Pan-Roasted Chicken with Garlic-Thyme Butter (page 193)—in fact, the combination was a knockout.

2 tablespoons unsalted butter

1 tablespoon olive oil

8 ounces carrots, cut into small dice

1 1/2 pounds large yellow squash, halved lengthwise and then sliced into 1/4-inch-thick half-moons

2 tablespoons thinly sliced shallot

1 1/2 teaspoons kosher salt

3/4 teaspoon freshly ground white pepper

1 tablespoon chopped fresh tarragon

1. Set a 12-inch sauté pan over medium-high heat, and once it is hot, add the butter and olive oil. When the butter has melted, add the carrots and cook, stirring often, for 2 minutes.

2. Add the yellow squash, shallot, salt, and white pepper to the pan and continue to cook, stirring often, until the squash has wilted and released most of its moisture, about 6 minutes. Sprinkle with the tarragon and toss to blend. Serve hot.

4 to 6 servings

ROASTED CARROTS WITH FRESH THYME

Prep time: 5 minutes **Cook time:** 10 to 12 minutes **Total:** 15 to 17 minutes

Carrots are an inexpensive, all-purpose root vegetable that are often overlooked. This delicious dish is a cinch to prepare and is easily jazzed up with any number of additions. Feel free to experiment by using different herbs, adding a handful of raisins, or drizzling with a splash of balsamic vinegar.

2 tablespoons olive oil

1$\frac{1}{2}$ pounds carrots, cut diagonally into 1$\frac{1}{2}$-inch lengths

1 teaspoon salt

$\frac{1}{2}$ teaspoon freshly ground black pepper

4 sprigs fresh thyme

2 tablespoons unsalted butter

1 tablespoon honey

1. Preheat the oven to 450°F.

2. Place a medium ovenproof sauté pan over high heat and add the olive oil. When the oil is hot, add the carrots, salt, and pepper and cook for 2 minutes on each side. Add the thyme sprigs and butter, and drizzle with the honey.

3. Transfer the pan to the oven and roast for 6 to 8 minutes, or until the carrots are golden and crisp-tender. Serve immediately.

4 servings

EMERIL'S SAUTÉED CUCUMBER WITH BASIL AND MINT

Prep time: 5 minutes **Cook time:** 12 minutes **Total:** 17 minutes

This is a great way to enjoy cucumbers—and one preparation that most folks don't think about when thinking cucumber. Delicate and buttery, these are especially wonderful alongside sautéed fish.

2 tablespoons butter

2 tablespoons olive oil

4 cups sliced peeled, seeded cucumber

1 tablespoon chopped fresh basil

1 tablespoon chopped fresh mint

1 teaspoon salt

$\frac{1}{2}$ teaspoon freshly ground black pepper

1 tablespoon freshly squeezed lime juice

1. Place a large sauté pan over medium-high heat, and add 1 tablespoon of the butter and 1 tablespoon of the olive oil. When the mixture is hot and bubbly, add 2 cups of the cucumbers. Cook until the cucumbers are lightly browned on one side, 2 to 3 minutes. Toss the cucumbers and brown on the other side, another 2 minutes. Add half of the basil, half of the mint, $\frac{1}{2}$ teaspoon of the salt, and $\frac{1}{4}$ teaspoon of the pepper. Transfer the cucumbers to a serving dish, and repeat the process with the remaining ingredients.

2. Drizzle the lime juice over the cucumbers, toss, and serve warm.

4 servings

GLAZED RADISHES

Prep time: 5 minutes **Cook time:** 15 minutes **Total:** 20 minutes

The end result of this unique preparation reminds me of turnips . . . we forget that radishes and turnips are close cousins. The pearly pink color really adds a wow factor to the dining table, too. A perfect side next to roast chicken or a simple sautéed fish fillet.

1½ pounds radishes, ends trimmed

2½ cups water

¼ cup sugar

2 tablespoons unsalted butter

1 teaspoon salt

½ teaspoon finely ground white pepper

4 teaspoons chopped fresh mint or tarragon

1. Cut the radishes into lengthwise quarters. Meanwhile, have a 12-inch sauté pan heating over medium heat.

2. Add the radishes to the hot pan and raise the heat to high. Carefully add the water, sugar, butter, salt, and white pepper (the liquids may splatter). Bring to a boil and cook, stirring occasionally, until the radishes are easily pierced with a fork and most of the liquid has evaporated, about 15 minutes.

3. Remove the radishes from the heat and sprinkle with the mint; toss to blend, and serve hot or warm.

4 servings

BROILED CATFISH WITH FRESH THYME, GARLIC, AND LEMON

Prep time: 10 minutes Cook time: 10 minutes **Total:** 20 minutes

There are two types of catfish I prefer: one is from the Mississippi Delta, where my wife's family is from, and the other is from Des Allemands, Louisiana, the self-proclaimed "catfish capital of the world." This is a very quick dish, and is always best when made with fresh catfish. However, if quality frozen catfish is available where you live, that'll work too.

Four 6- to 8-ounce skinless catfish fillets

2 teaspoons Emeril's Original Essence or Creole Seasoning (page 29)

$1/2$ teaspoon salt

$1/4$ teaspoon freshly ground white pepper

1 tablespoon minced garlic

3 tablespoons extra-virgin olive oil

1 teaspoon fresh thyme leaves

Juice of 1 lemon

1 tablespoon chopped fresh parsley (optional)

Lemon wedges, for serving (optional)

1. Position a rack about 4 inches from the broiler element and preheat the broiler.

2. Line a rimmed baking sheet with aluminum foil. Season the catfish fillets on both sides with the Essence, salt, and white pepper, and place the fillets on the prepared baking sheet.

3. In a small bowl, combine the garlic, olive oil, and thyme. Using a small spoon, spread the garlic mixture evenly over the catfish. Then drizzle the fillets with the lemon juice.

4. Transfer the baking sheet to the broiler. Cook the catfish for 6 minutes. Then rotate the baking sheet front to back, and continue cooking until the fish flakes easily when pressed with your fingers at the thickest part, about 4 minutes longer.

5. Remove from the oven and serve immediately, sprinkled with the parsley and garnished with lemon wedges if desired.

4 servings

BROILED SALMON WITH A WARM TOMATO-LEMON VINAIGRETTE

Prep time: 6 minutes **Cook time:** 9 minutes **Total:** 15 minutes

Most people really enjoy salmon because of its "steak-like" texture and wonderful flavor. Wait until you try it with a tomato-lemon vinaigrette! Oh, baby, this is not only tasty but healthy and beautiful, too.

. . . .

¼ cup plus 1 tablespoon extra-virgin olive oil

1 tablespoon fresh marjoram leaves

½ teaspoon finely grated lemon zest

2 cups cherry tomatoes, halved

1½ teaspoons salt

¾ teaspoon freshly ground black pepper

¼ cup freshly squeezed lemon juice

Four 6-ounce salmon fillets

1. Position a rack 6 to 8 inches from the broiler element and preheat the broiler. Line a rimmed baking sheet with parchment paper.

2. Heat the ¼ cup olive oil in a 10-inch sauté pan over high heat. When it is hot, add the marjoram and lemon zest and cook until fragrant, about 15 seconds. Add the tomatoes, ½ teaspoon of the salt, and ¼ teaspoon of the pepper. Cook until the tomatoes begin to wilt, about 2 minutes. Stir in the lemon juice and mix well. Remove from the heat and set aside.

3. Arrange the salmon fillets on the prepared baking sheet. Brush the fillets with the remaining 1 tablespoon olive oil and season with the remaining 1 teaspoon salt and ½ teaspoon pepper. Broil until the salmon is browned and cooked through, 5 to 6 minutes.

4. Remove from the oven, and serve with the tomato-lemon vinaigrette spooned over the top.

4 servings

GAAAHLICKY SIZZLING SHRIMP

Prep time: 10 minutes **Cook time:** 4 to 5 minutes **Total:** 14 to 15 minutes

Garlic meets shrimp. This is really simple and equally delicious eaten over pasta, over steamed white rice or creamy grits, or over nothing at all, with crusty French bread for sopping up all the garlicky goodness.

2 pounds medium shrimp, peeled and deveined

2 teaspoons Emeril's Original Essence or Creole Seasoning (page 29)

1/2 teaspoon salt

2 tablespoons olive oil

2 tablespoons unsalted butter

2 tablespoons roughly chopped garlic

6 tablespoons shrimp or chicken stock or canned, low-sodium shrimp or chicken broth

2 tablespoons freshly squeezed lemon juice

1 tablespoon chopped fresh parsley

1. In a medium bowl, toss the shrimp with the Essence and the salt. Set aside.

2. Heat a large cast-iron pan over medium-high heat, and add the olive oil. When the oil is hot, add the butter and garlic. Once the butter is nearly melted (about 20 seconds), add the shrimp and cook, stirring occasionally, until they are cooked through, about 3 minutes.

3. Add the stock, lemon juice, and parsley, and cook for 30 seconds. Remove from the heat. Serve immediately.

2 to 4 servings

SOUTHERN-STYLE PAN-FRIED CATFISH

Prep time: 12 minutes **Cook time:** 8 minutes **Total:** 20 minutes

A quintessential Southern dish. If you're not from the South, here's your chance to transport your guests to a place they may never have been to. If you are a Southerner, you will arrive in a place that's nostalgic and new all at once. Delicious.

1/2 cup buttermilk

2 tablespoons whole-grain mustard

1 tablespoon Emeril's Original Essence or Creole Seasoning (page 29)

1 tablespoon minced garlic

2 teaspoons Louisiana hot sauce or other red hot sauce

Four 6- to 8-ounce skinless catfish fillets

1 cup all-purpose flour

2/3 cup cornmeal

1 tablespoon salt

2/3 cup vegetable oil, for frying

Kicked-Up Tartar Sauce (recipe follows), for serving, optional

Lemon wedges, for serving

1. Whisk together the buttermilk, mustard, Essence, garlic, and hot sauce in a small bowl. Place the fillets in a tray or baking dish that is just big enough to hold them. Pour the buttermilk mixture over the fish, making sure they are evenly coated. Set aside to marinate while you assemble the remaining ingredients.

2. In a second tray or shallow baking dish, whisk together the flour, cornmeal, and salt.

3. One at a time, remove the fillets from the buttermilk mixture, allowing any excess to drip off. Transfer the fish to the flour-cornmeal mixture and dredge to evenly coat. Place the breaded fish on a plate, and set aside.

4. Heat the vegetable oil in a large sauté pan over medium heat. When the oil is hot, carefully add 2 fillets to the pan, presentation side down, and cook until they are golden brown and crisp, about 4 minutes. Turn and cook until golden on the second side, 3 to 4 minutes. Using a fish spatula, transfer the fillets to a paper towel–lined plate. Repeat with the remaining 2 fillets.

5. Serve hot, with the Kicked-Up Tartar Sauce and lemon wedges, if desired, alongside.

4 servings

Kicked-Up Tartar Sauce

Prep time: 10 minutes Total: 10 minutes

We wouldn't just give you any ole tartar sauce recipe. Creole mustard, hot sauce, cayenne, and tarragon. . . . Quick to whip up and definitely worth the effort. Heinz who?

1 cup mayonnaise
$1/4$ cup finely chopped cornichons, dill pickles, or dill
   pickle relish, drained
2 tablespoons minced shallots
2 tablespoons minced green onion tops
1 tablespoon finely chopped drained nonpareil capers
1 tablespoon chopped fresh parsley
2 teaspoons Creole mustard or other spicy
   whole-grain mustard
$1/2$ teaspoon Louisiana hot sauce
$1/4$ teaspoon cayenne pepper
$1/4$ teaspoon dried tarragon, crushed between your
   fingers

Combine all the ingredients in a small bowl and stir well to blend. Refrigerate until ready to serve. This will keep for 1 week.

About 1$1/2$ cups

BLUE CORN–CRUSTED RAINBOW TROUT WITH CILANTRO-LIME SOUR CREAM

Prep time: 8 minutes **Cook time:** 6 minutes **Total:** 14 minutes

You'd better make extra batches of this dish—my Culinary Team couldn't keep their hands off it when we tested it in our kitchen! Before I knew it, the fish was long gone and not even a crumb was left on the plate.

. . . .

$1/_2$ cup sour cream

1 tablespoon chopped fresh cilantro

1 tablespoon freshly squeezed lime juice

$1/_4$ teaspoon cayenne pepper

$1 1/_4$ teaspoons salt

Generous $1/_2$ teaspoon plus $1/_8$ teaspoon freshly ground black pepper

1 cup blue cornmeal

1 teaspoon ground coriander

1 teaspoon ground cumin

Four 6-ounce skinless rainbow trout fillets

4 tablespoons vegetable oil

2 tablespoons butter

Lime wedges, for serving

1. Combine the sour cream, cilantro, lime juice, cayenne pepper, $1/_4$ teaspoon of the salt, and the $1/_8$ teaspoon black pepper in a small bowl and stir to mix well. Set aside.

2. Combine the blue cornmeal with the coriander and cumin in a shallow dish, and whisk to blend.

3. Season the fish fillets on both sides with the remaining 1 teaspoon salt and generous $1/_2$ teaspoon black pepper. Then dredge them in the blue cornmeal mixture, shaking to remove any excess.

4. Heat 2 tablespoons of the vegetable oil in a large nonstick sauté pan over medium-high heat. When it is hot, add 1 tablespoon of the butter. When the butter has melted, add 2 fillets, underside down, and cook until the skin side is golden brown and crisp, 2 to 3 minutes. Flip the fillets over and cook briefly on the presentation side until the fish is just cooked through, 1 to 2 minutes. Remove from the pan and keep warm. Wipe the pan clean, add the remaining 2 tablespoons oil and 1 tablespoon butter, and repeat with the remaining fillets.

5. Serve each fillet with a dollop of the cilantro-lime sour cream, and garnish with lime wedges.

4 servings

TROUT À LA MEUNIÈRE

Prep time: 10 minutes **Cook time:** 10 minutes **Total:** 20 minutes

This is a classic New Orleans dish in which thin trout fillets are dredged in flour, then quickly sautéed and finished with a simple lemony butter sauce. Any fresh trout from the gulf, the brook, or da bayou will do.

Four 6-ounce skinless trout fillets

1 teaspoon salt, plus more to taste

1 teaspoon Emeril's Original Essence or Creole Seasoning (page 29)

½ cup Wondra flour (see Note)

4 tablespoons olive oil

8 tablespoons (1 stick) unsalted butter, cubed, at room temperature

1 tablespoon minced shallot

2 tablespoons dry white wine

2 tablespoons freshly squeezed lemon juice

½ cup thinly sliced almonds

2 tablespoons chopped fresh parsley

Freshly ground white pepper

1. Preheat the oven to 200°F.

2. Season the trout fillets with the salt and the Essence. Lightly dredge the seasoned trout in the Wondra, shaking to remove any excess.

3. Set a 10-inch sauté pan over medium-high heat and add 2 tablespoons of the olive oil. Once the oil is hot, place 2 fish fillets in the pan and cook until golden, about 2 minutes per side. Place the cooked fillets on an ovenproof serving platter and keep warm in the oven while you cook the remaining fillets in the same manner with the remaining 2 tablespoons of olive oil.

4. Once all the fillets are cooked, return the empty sauté pan to the stovetop and reduce the heat to medium. Add the butter to the pan, and when it has melted, add the shallot. Cook for 30 seconds. Then add the white wine, lemon juice, almonds, and parsley. Continue to cook for 30 to 40 seconds, swirling the pan occasionally. Season the sauce with salt and white pepper to taste, and remove from the heat.

5. Remove the platter from the oven, pour the sauce over the fish, and serve immediately.

Note: Wondra is an instant flour most typically used for sauce because it dissolves quickly. We have found that its fine texture is perfect for a thin crisp coating on seared fish.

4 servings

CLASSIC MOULES MARINIÈRE

Prep time: 10 minutes **Cook time:** 8 minutes **Total:** 18 minutes

A classic white wine–based dish, with a touch of cream and lots of shallots and garlic. In the Provençal region of France, they add tomatoes to this dish; feel free to do so if you like. You can enjoy this with either crusty bread or toasted slices of French bread, as in the Bruschetta recipe on page 11. In French bistros, these mussels are traditionally served with *pommes frites*.

3 tablespoons unsalted butter

6 tablespoons chopped shallots

1 tablespoon minced garlic

2 sprigs fresh parsley, plus 2 tablespoons chopped fresh parsley for garnish

2 sprigs fresh thyme

1 cup dry white wine

$1/4$ cup heavy cream

$1/2$ teaspoon salt

$1/2$ teaspoon freshly ground black pepper

4 pounds (about 4 dozen) live mussels, well scrubbed, rinsed, and debearded

Crusty French bread, for serving

1. In a large deep sauté pan or a large wide saucepan, melt the butter over medium-high heat. Add the shallots, garlic, and herb sprigs and cook, stirring, until the shallots are soft and fragrant, about 1 minute. Add the wine, heavy cream, salt, and pepper, and bring to a boil.

2. Add the mussels, cover the pan, and cook, shaking the pan occasionally, until the mussels have opened, 5 to 6 minutes.

3. Remove the pan from the heat and discard any mussels that have not opened. Transfer the mussels and their liquid to a large, deep serving bowl and garnish with the chopped parsley. Serve immediately, with French bread for dipping.

4 servings

STIR-FRIED CHICKEN WITH CASHEWS

Prep time: 12 minutes **Cook time:** 6 minutes **Total:** 18 minutes

Hoisin sauce is a Chinese condiment that is easy to find in most supermarkets; its distinct flavor really makes this dish come alive. If you'd like, feel free to substitute an equal amount of shrimp or turkey for the chicken. This dish would be right at home served with the Aromatic Jasmine Rice on page 57.

½ cup plus 2 teaspoons chicken stock or canned, low-sodium chicken broth

¼ cup hoisin sauce

2 tablespoons soy sauce

3 tablespoons vegetable oil

1¼ pounds boneless, skinless chicken breasts, cut crosswise into ½-inch-thick even slices

¼ cup finely chopped green onion bottoms, plus 2 tablespoons thinly sliced green onion tops

2 teaspoons minced garlic

½ teaspoon crushed red pepper, or to taste

1 large red bell pepper, stemmed, seeded, and julienned (see page 7)

1 teaspoon cornstarch

½ cup roasted cashews

Salt and freshly ground black pepper

Cooked white rice, for serving

1. In a small bowl, combine the ½ cup chicken broth, the hoisin sauce, and the soy sauce. Set this sauce aside.

2. Heat the oil in a wok or a large sauté pan over high heat. When the oil is hot, add the chicken and cook until it just turns opaque, 2 to 3 minutes. Add the green onion bottoms, garlic, and crushed red pepper and cook until fragrant, about 30 seconds. Add the red bell pepper and cook until just tender, about 1 minute.

3. Add the sauce to the pan and mix well. In a small bowl, combine the cornstarch with the remaining 2 teaspoons chicken broth and stir well. Add the cornstarch mixture to the stir-fry and bring to a boil. Continue to simmer until the sauce begins to thicken, about 45 seconds.

4. Remove from the heat and stir in the green onion tops and cashews. Season with salt and pepper to taste. Serve over cooked white rice.

About 4 servings

SAUTÉED CHICKEN BREASTS WITH DIJON HERB SAUCE

Prep time: 6 minutes **Cook time:** 14 minutes **Total:** 20 minutes

Simply described, this dish is a classic! Serve it with a green salad and hot, crusty, buttered bread. Don't make me say it: "plate-lickin' good"!

Four 6- to 8-ounce boneless, skinless chicken breasts

1 teaspoon salt

1/2 teaspoon freshly ground white pepper

2 tablespoons olive oil

2 tablespoons chopped shallot

1 cup dry white wine

1 tablespoon Dijon mustard

1/2 cup heavy cream

1 teaspoon chopped fresh tarragon

1 teaspoon chopped fresh parsley

1. Season the chicken on both sides with the salt and white pepper. Heat the olive oil in a 12-inch sauté pan over medium-high heat. Place the chicken in the pan, and cook until golden, about 4 minutes per side.

2. Increase the heat to high, add the shallot and white wine, and cook for 4 minutes. Remove the chicken and set it aside on a serving plate.

3. Whisk the mustard and heavy cream into the pan, and bring the sauce to a boil. Then reduce the heat to medium and simmer for 2 minutes, until thickened and bubbly.

4. Add the tarragon and parsley, and remove from the heat. Spoon the sauce over the chicken, and serve immediately.

4 servings

CHICKEN SALAD WITH FRESH HERBS AND CELERY

Prep time: 8 minutes **Cook time:** 12 minutes **Total:** 20 minutes

This delicious chicken salad is a breeze to put together, especially if you make the most of your time by prepping the dressing and chopped ingredients while the chicken is roasting in the oven. Feel free to make this up to two days in advance. Serve it in sandwiches or with greens for a light salad entrée.

. . . .

2 pounds boneless, skinless chicken breasts

2 teaspoons salt

1/2 teaspoon freshly ground black pepper

2 tablespoons olive oil

1 cup mayonnaise

1 teaspoon minced garlic

1/2 teaspoon Dijon mustard

1/2 cup finely diced celery, plus 1/4 cup chopped celery leaves

1/3 cup finely chopped red onion

3 tablespoons chopped mixed fresh herbs (such as parsley and tarragon)

1/2 teaspoon celery seeds

1/4 teaspoon cayenne pepper

1. Preheat the oven to 400°F.

2. Rinse the chicken briefly under cool running water, then pat dry with paper towels. Season on both sides with the salt and pepper.

3. Heat the olive oil in a 12-inch ovenproof sauté pan over high heat. Add the chicken to the pan and cook for 2 minutes. Turn the chicken over and immediately place the pan in the oven. Roast for 10 minutes, or until the chicken reaches an internal temperature of 165°F when tested with an instant-read thermometer. Remove from the oven and set aside to cool.

4. In a large mixing bowl, combine the mayonnaise, garlic, mustard, celery, celery leaves, red onion, herbs, celery seeds, and cayenne pepper. Mix well.

5. When the chicken is cool enough to handle, cut it into 1/2-inch dice, add it to the mayonnaise mixture, and mix well. Serve immediately, or transfer to the refrigerator to chill.

4 to 6 servings

LAMB T-BONES WITH ROSEMARY-BALSAMIC BUTTER SAUCE

Prep time: 6 minutes **Cook time:** 14 minutes **Total:** 20 minutes

You don't have to go to a restaurant to have great lamb chops. People assume that lamb is difficult to cook, or too fancy to cook at home, but wait until you see how easy these little T-bones are.

Eight 2-inch-thick lamb T-bone chops (about 2 pounds)

$1/4$ cup plus 2 teaspoons olive oil

$1/2$ cup balsamic vinegar

2 teaspoons minced garlic

$1^1/2$ tablespoons chopped fresh rosemary

$1/2$ teaspoon salt

2 shallots

$1/2$ cup dry red wine

6 tablespoons ($3/4$ stick) butter, cut into medium dice

$1/2$ teaspoon coarse sea salt

$1/4$ teaspoon freshly ground black pepper

1. Place the lamb chops in a gallon-size resealable plastic bag. In a small bowl, combine the $1/4$ cup olive oil, $1/4$ cup of the balsamic vinegar, the garlic, $1/2$ tablespoon of the rosemary, and the salt; stir together with a fork. Pour the marinade into the bag with the lamb chops, seal, and set aside at room temperature while you prepare the remaining ingredients.

2. Mince the shallots (about 2 tablespoons), and place them in an 8-inch skillet. Add the red wine and remaining $1/4$ cup balsamic vinegar, and bring to a boil over medium-high heat. Cook until the mixture has reduced to a syrupy consistency and the entire surface of the sauce is bubbly, 7 to 8 minutes. Reduce the heat to low and whisk in the butter in three separate additions, fully incorporating each addition before adding more; do not allow the sauce to boil. Add the remaining 1 tablespoon rosemary, remove from the heat, and set aside. (Keep the sauce warm, covered, until ready to serve but do not allow it to boil.)

3. Remove the lamb chops from the marinade, lightly pat them dry with a paper towel, and set them on a plate. Season both sides of the chops with the sea salt and black pepper. Heat the remaining 2 teaspoons olive oil in a 10-inch sauté pan over medium-high heat. When the oil is hot, add the chops and cook for 3 minutes. Reduce the heat to medium, turn the chops over, and cook for 3 minutes for medium-rare. Set the chops aside to rest briefly before serving.

4. Serve the chops drizzled with the rosemary-balsamic butter sauce.

4 servings

STEAK AU POIVRE

Prep time: 5 minutes Cook time: 15 minutes Total: 20 minutes

In a classic steak au poivre, peppercorns are coarsely crushed by hand using the bottom of a skillet . . . but in this quick and easy version, the pepper is simply coarsely ground in a peppermill. The pepper coating on the outside of the steaks roasts in a hot, dry cast-iron skillet, drawing out the natural oils from the peppercorns and imparting a deep flavor. The cream and brandy finish the dish with just the right richness.

¼ cup coarsely ground black pepper

Two 2-inch-thick rib-eye steaks (about 1 pound each)

1½ teaspoons kosher salt

¼ cup brandy or cognac

2 tablespoons Worcestershire sauce

1 tablespoon freshly squeezed lemon juice

½ cup heavy cream

2 tablespoons butter

2 teaspoons chopped fresh parsley

1. Sprinkle the pepper over both sides of the steaks, and gently press it into the meat with the heel of your hand.

2. Sprinkle the salt over the bottom of a large cast-iron skillet. Heat the skillet over high heat. When the salt begins to brown, add the steaks. Lower the heat to medium-high and cook, without disturbing, for 5 minutes. Turn the steaks over and cook for 5 minutes more.

3. Carefully add the brandy or cognac to the pan, taking care as it may ignite (allow the flames to burn off). Transfer the steaks to a platter to set aside to rest.

4. Add the Worcestershire, lemon juice, and cream to the skillet and cook for 1 minute. Then whisk in the butter. Remove the pan from the heat, and stir in the parsley. Spoon the sauce over the steaks, and serve immediately.

Notes: If you prefer a higher degree of doneness, preheat the oven to 400°F. After browning the steaks on both sides, transfer then to a baking sheet and place it in the oven to cook further while you finish the sauce in the skillet.

For thinner steaks: Change the cook time to 3 minutes per side for 1-inch rib-eyes.

For a lighter version of this sauce: substitute ¼ cup beef broth for ¼ cup of the cream.

2 to 4 servings

NEW YORK STRIP WITH BEURRE MAÎTRE D'HÔTEL

Prep time: 5 minutes **Inactive time:** 5 minutes **Cook time:** 12 to 14 minutes
Total: 22 to 24 minutes

Whoa! You're pulling out all the stops here! Gorgeously seared New York strips with a slab of flavorful butter, on the table in fifteen minutes! Pour the wine and pass the salad.

8 ounces (2 sticks) unsalted butter, at room temperature

$1/4$ cup minced fresh parsley

3 teaspoons freshly squeezed lemon juice

$4^1/2$ teaspoons salt

$2^1/4$ teaspoons freshly ground black pepper

Four 12- to 14-ounce boneless New York strip steaks, fat trimmed

4 teaspoons olive oil

1. Preheat the oven to 450°F.

2. Place the butter in a medium bowl. Add the parsley, lemon juice, $1/2$ teaspoon of the salt, and $1/4$ teaspoon of the pepper, and stir until combined. Refrigerate while you cook the steaks.

3. Heat a large cast-iron skillet over medium-high heat.

4. Rub both sides of the steaks with the olive oil, and season evenly with the remaining 4 teaspoons salt and 2 teaspoons pepper. Place the steaks in the hot skillet and cook for 4 minutes on each side. Then transfer the skillet to the oven and roast to the desired degree of doneness, 4 to 6 minutes for medium-rare. An instant-read thermometer inserted into the thickest part of the meat should register 130°F for medium-rare, 140°F for medium.

5. Remove the skillet from the oven; let the steaks stand for 5 minutes before serving.

6. When ready to serve, top the steaks with spoonfuls of the flavored butter, to taste, or slice the steaks crosswise into $1/3$-inch-thick slices and serve with the butter. (Any unused butter can be stored in an airtight container in the refrigerator for up to 1 week.)

4 to 6 servings

LAMB CHOPS WITH MUSTARD HERB CRUST

Prep time: 9 minutes **Cook time:** 11 minutes **Total:** 20 minutes

Sear. Slather. Coat. Roast. Eat. Impress your friends with this one.

. . . .

½ cup Dijon mustard

2 tablespoons minced garlic

1 cup unseasoned dry breadcrumbs

¼ cup finely grated Parmigiano-
    Reggiano cheese

¼ cup chopped fresh rosemary

2 teaspoons dried Italian herbs

2 tablespoons vegetable oil

Sixteen 2- to 3-ounce baby lamb
    chops

2 teaspoons salt

1 teaspoon freshly ground black
    pepper

1. Preheat the broiler, and line a large baking sheet with aluminum foil.

2. Combine the mustard and garlic in a small mixing bowl, and set aside. Combine the breadcrumbs, cheese, rosemary, and dried herbs in a shallow dish; whisk to mix well, and set aside.

3. Heat the vegetable oil in a large sauté pan over medium-high heat. Using a paper towel, pat the lamb chops dry. Season them with the salt and pepper. Add the lamb chops to the pan and sear on both sides until nicely browned and caramelized, about 2 minutes per side.

4. Transfer the chops to a plate and using a basting brush, lightly coat them with the mustard mixture. Then dredge them in the breadcrumb mixture. As the chops are coated, transfer them to the prepared baking sheet. Place the baking sheet under the broiler, and cook until the chops develop a nice golden crust and reach an internal temperature of 145°F when tested with an instant-read thermometer, about 5 minutes.

5. Remove the baking sheet from the oven and let the lamb chops rest for 5 minutes before serving.

4 main-course servings

MINUTE STEAKS TERIYAKI-STYLE

Prep time: 10 minutes **Cook time:** 10 minutes **Total:** 20 minutes

You will not believe this stir-fry! Portion your meat, slice your onions, peppers, and carrots, cook it all over high heat, and finish with the sauce. Done.

. . . .

2 pounds top sirloin steak,
$\frac{1}{4}$ inch thick, cut into 6 or 8
portions

$\frac{3}{4}$ cup soy sauce

6 tablespoons rice wine vinegar

$\frac{1}{4}$ cup chopped green onions,
white and green parts

2 tablespoons sugar

2 teaspoons chopped garlic

1 teaspoon cornstarch

$\frac{1}{2}$ teaspoon crushed red pepper

3 tablespoons vegetable oil

1$\frac{1}{2}$ cups thinly sliced onions

1 medium bell pepper, thinly sliced
(about 1 cup)

1 medium carrot, halved lengthwise
and thinly sliced (about 1 cup)

Steamed white rice, for serving
(optional)

1. Place the sirloin in a resealable plastic bag, add $\frac{1}{2}$ cup of the soy sauce, seal, and set aside for 10 minutes.

2. While the steaks are marinating, make your sauce: In a small bowl, combine the remaining $\frac{1}{4}$ cup soy sauce, vinegar, green onions, sugar, garlic, cornstarch, and crushed red pepper. Set aside.

3. Remove the steaks from the marinade, lightly pat them dry, and set them aside on a plate.

4. Heat 2 tablespoons of the vegetable oil in a 12-inch sauté pan over medium-high heat. Add half of the steaks and cook until nicely browned, 1$\frac{1}{2}$ minutes per side. Transfer them to a serving platter, and repeat with the remaining steaks.

5. Add the remaining 1 tablespoon vegetable oil to the pan, and when it is hot, add the onions, bell pepper, and carrot. Cook, stirring occasionally, until crisp-tender, 3 minutes. Stir the sauce, add it to the pan, and cook for 1 minute longer. Spoon the vegetables and sauce over the steaks. Serve immediately, over steamed white rice if desired.

4 to 6 servings

BONELESS PORK CHOPS PARMIGIANA

Prep time: 10 minutes **Cook time:** 10 minutes **Total:** 20 minutes

Everyone knows how delicious Chicken Parmesan can be, but I decided to do a spin-off with pork. Your friends and family will be astonished at how quickly this dish comes together.

. . . .

2 pounds boneless thin-cut pork chops (about 8 small chops)

1 teaspoon salt

$1/2$ teaspoon freshly ground black pepper

$1/4$ cup all-purpose flour

1 egg

2 tablespoons milk

1 cup fine dry unseasoned bread crumbs

$1/2$ cup finely grated Parmigiano-Reggiano cheese

4 teaspoons Emeril's Original Essence or Creole Seasoning (page 29)

$1/2$ cup olive oil

1 cup jarred marinara sauce, plus more (heated) for serving with pasta if desired

2 cups grated mozzarella cheese

Cooked pasta, for serving (optional)

1. Preheat the broiler, and line a large baking sheet with aluminum foil.

2. Season the pork chops on both sides with the salt and pepper. Set three shallow pans side by side. Place the flour in one, the egg and milk in another, and the breadcrumbs and cheese in the third pan. Season the flour with $1^1/2$ teaspoons of the Essence, the egg-milk mixture with $1^1/2$ teaspoons of the Essence, and the breadcrumbs with 1 teaspoon of the Essence. Stir the flour to incorporate the Essence; beat the eggs, milk, and Essence to blend; and toss the breadcrumbs with the cheese and Essence to combine.

3. Dredge the pork chops in the flour and shake to remove any excess. Working with one at a time, dip the pork chops in the egg wash to coat, then transfer them to the breadcrumb mixture and coat evenly, shaking to remove any excess.

4. Set a 12-inch sauté pan over medium-high heat and add the olive oil. When the oil is hot, place half of the breaded pork chops in the pan and cook until golden brown, $1^1/2$ to 2 minutes per side. Transfer the browned pork chops to the prepared baking sheet. Repeat with the remaining pork chops.

5. Spread 2 tablespoons of the marinara sauce over each of the pork chops, and top each with $1/4$ cup of

the grated mozzarella. Place the baking sheet under the broiler and cook for 2 to 2$\frac{1}{2}$ minutes, until the cheese is bubbly and lightly browned in spots and the chops are just cooked through. Remove from the oven and, if desired, serve over cooked pasta with additional marinara sauce.

8 cutlets, 4 to 6 servings

SPICY PORK STIR-FRY WITH GREEN BEANS

Prep time: 12 minutes **Cook time:** 8 minutes **Total:** 20 minutes

Nowadays you can easily find fresh, beautiful, washed packaged green beans. Grab 'em and go. Here is a quick and delicious way to serve them.

3 tablespoons soy sauce

1/4 teaspoon freshly ground white pepper

1 pound ground pork

1/4 cup chicken stock or canned, low-sodium chicken broth

3 1/2 tablespoons hoisin sauce

1/2 teaspoon crushed red pepper

1 tablespoon rice wine vinegar

1/2 teaspoon cornstarch

1/4 cup peanut oil

12 ounces green beans, rinsed, ends trimmed, cut into 4-inch lengths

3 tablespoons thinly sliced garlic

1 1/2 teaspoons dark Asian sesame oil

Cooked white rice, for serving (optional)

1. In a mixing bowl, combine 2 tablespoons of the soy sauce, the white pepper, and the ground pork. Mix well to combine, and then set aside.

2. Make the sauce by combining the chicken stock, hoisin sauce, crushed red pepper, rice vinegar, cornstarch, and the remaining 1 tablespoon soy sauce in a bowl. Set aside.

3. Heat a wok or sauté pan over high heat until hot. Add the peanut oil, and when the oil is smoking, add the green beans and cook, stirring frequently, until they are slightly wrinkled, 3 to 5 minutes. Using a slotted spoon, transfer the beans to a paper towel–lined plate, and set aside.

4. Add the garlic to the wok and cook briefly until fragrant, about 10 seconds. Add the ground pork and stir-fry until it is no longer pink, about 1 1/2 minutes. Stir the sauce mixture, add it to the wok, and stir to combine. Bring the liquid to a boil and cook until it begins to thicken, about 45 seconds.

5. Return the green beans to the wok and drizzle with the sesame oil. Cook briefly until warmed through. Then serve immediately, over hot rice if desired.

4 servings

MUSHROOM-SMOTHERED STEAKS

Prep time: 10 minutes **Cook time:** 10 minutes **Total:** 20 minutes

Cube steaks, also referred to as minute steaks, are not cubes at all. They are called cube steaks because of the cubelike pattern that has been pounded into them with a meat tenderizer. These steaks can be cooked very quickly, will remain tender and juicy, and are very affordable . . . need I say more?

4 cube steaks (about 1½ pounds total)

¾ teaspoon salt

¾ teaspoon freshly ground black pepper

4 tablespoons olive oil

1 pound mushrooms, wiped clean, stemmed, and sliced (about 4 cups)

½ cup chopped green onions, white and green parts, plus more for garnish

1½ tablespoons minced garlic

½ cup dry red wine

3 tablespoons butter, cut into 4 pieces

1. Season the steaks on both sides with ½ teaspoon of the salt and ½ teaspoon of the black pepper.

2. Heat 2 tablespoons of the olive oil in a 14-inch sauté pan over medium-high heat. Add the steaks and cook until nicely browned on one side, 2 minutes. Remove from the pan and set aside.

3. Add the remaining 2 tablespoons olive oil to the pan. Then add the mushrooms, green onions, and garlic and sauté until browned, about 2 minutes. Move the mushrooms to the edge of the pan and return the steaks, browned sides up, along with any accumulated juices, to the pan. Add the wine and cook for 3 minutes. Add the remaining ¼ teaspoon salt and ¼ teaspoon black pepper. Dot each steak with a pat of butter and cook for 1 minute longer.

4. Transfer the steaks to a serving platter or individual plates, and spoon the mushrooms and their juices over them. Sprinkle with chopped green onions and serve immediately.

4 servings

EMERIL'S LATE-NIGHT PARFAITS

Prep time: 7 minutes (including 5 minutes inactive) **Total:** 7 minutes

The great thing about these parfaits is that they can be assembled and ready in no time. Don't worry if you don't have the exact ingredients called for; any type of cookie and ice cream you have on hand can work wonderfully together.

1 pint vanilla ice cream

½ cup crumbled biscotti cookies or other cookie crumbs of choice

¼ cup Frangelico or other nut-flavored liqueur

2 tablespoons roughly chopped hazelnuts or walnuts, lightly toasted

1. Remove the ice cream from the freezer and let it soften slightly, about 5 minutes at room temperature.

2. Into the bottom of four parfait or ice cream dishes, scoop about 2 tablespoons of the vanilla ice cream. Top with about ½ tablespoon of the cookie crumbs, and drizzle with 1½ teaspoons of the liqueur. Continue layering the ingredients, ending with liqueur on top.

3. Serve immediately, garnished with the chopped nuts.

4 servings

BROWN SUGAR–BAKED BANANAS

Prep time: 10 minutes **Cook time:** 8 minutes **Total:** 18 minutes

In New Orleans we have a classic dessert known as Bananas Foster. This simplified oven-baked version is every bit as good, but oh, what a walk in the park to prepare.

2 tablespoons unsalted butter

3 bananas, peeled, sliced in half lengthwise and crosswise

1/3 cup packed light brown sugar

1/2 teaspoon ground cinnamon

1/4 teaspoon freshly grated nutmeg

Juice of 1 orange

1/4 teaspoon grated orange zest

Light rum or banana liqueur, for drizzling (optional)

Vanilla ice cream, for serving

1. Position a rack about 8 inches from the broiler element and preheat the broiler to high.

2. Butter the bottom of a flameproof 11- by 7-inch baking dish with 1 tablespoon of the butter, and arrange the banana slices in it in one even layer, cut sides down. Set aside.

3. In a small saucepan over medium-high heat, combine the remaining 1 tablespoon butter with the brown sugar, cinnamon, nutmeg, and orange juice. Cook, stirring, until the sugar begins to melt, 1 to 2 minutes. Remove from the heat and stir in the orange zest. Pour the sauce evenly over the bananas.

4. Place the baking dish under the broiler and cook, turning the bananas over midway through, until the sauce is slightly thickened and bubbly and the bananas are tender, about 6 minutes total.

5. Remove the baking dish from the broiler, and if desired, drizzle with rum. Set aside to cool briefly before serving.

6. Serve the bananas over vanilla ice cream, with some of the sauce drizzled over the top.

4 servings

CANDIED HOT FUDGE SUNDAES

Prep time: 15 minutes **Cook time:** 5 minutes **Total:** 20 minutes

Decadent and delightful . . .

¾ cup heavy cream

¼ cup light corn syrup

½ cup semisweet chocolate chips

2 tablespoons unsalted butter

½ teaspoon vanilla extract

3 ounces (about ¾ cup) of your favorite chocolate–peanut butter candy bar (such as Reese's Peanut Butter Cups or Snickers bars), coarsely chopped

2 large ripe bananas, peeled and sliced

Vanilla ice cream, for serving

1½ cups lightly sweetened whipped cream, for serving (optional)

Crushed roasted salted peanuts, for garnish

6 maraschino cherries, for garnish

1. Carefully heat the heavy cream and corn syrup in a small saucepan. When the mixture is hot, remove the pan from the heat, add the chocolate chips, and let sit undisturbed for about 3 minutes.

2. Whisk the cream mixture until smooth, and return the saucepan to low heat. Warm, stirring the sauce frequently, until it is heated through, 1 to 2 minutes. Add the butter in pieces, stirring until incorporated and smooth. Remove from the heat and let sit for 1 minute to cool. Then stir in the vanilla extract and chocolate candy bar pieces.

3. Divide the sliced bananas equally among six sundae glasses or ice cream dishes. Spoon the chocolate sauce over the bananas, then top with scoops of ice cream. Place a dollop of whipped cream over the top, if desired, and then sprinkle with roasted peanuts. Top each sundae with a cherry and serve immediately.

6 servings

PEANUT BUTTER-CHOCOLATE CHIP COOKIES

Prep time: 5 minutes **Cook time:** 10 minutes **Total:** 15 minutes

These are by far the easiest and best-tasting peanut butter cookies you will ever make. A perfect recipe for kids—no fuss, no muss.

. . . .

1 cup creamy peanut butter

$1/2$ cup granulated sugar

$1/2$ cup packed light brown sugar

$1/2$ cup semisweet chocolate chips

1 large egg, beaten

1 teaspoon vanilla extract

1. Position two oven racks in the center of the oven and preheat the oven to 350°F.

2. Combine all the ingredients in a bowl, and stir with a wooden spoon until smooth.

3. Divide the dough into 24 portions, about 1 heaping tablespoon each. Roll each portion between your hands to form a smooth ball. Place the balls of dough on ungreased cookie sheets, spacing them 1 inch apart. You should get about 12 cookies per sheet. Using a fork, press on the dough in two directions to form a crosshatch pattern.

4. Bake the cookies, rotating the sheets between oven racks and turning them back to front midway, until the cookies are puffed and lightly golden, about 10 minutes. Remove the baking sheets from the oven and let the cookies cool on the sheets. Then remove them with a metal spatula.

About 24 cookies

MELON WITH AMARETTI COOKIE CRUMBLES

Prep time: 10 minutes **Inactive time:** 5 to 10 minutes **Total:** 15 to 20 minutes

This recipe relies on the ripeness of your fruit and is best prepared when melons are in season. Tip: If the melons you purchase are not ripe when you buy them, place them in a brown paper bag, add a banana, seal the bag, and set aside for a day or two.

1 ripe honeydew melon, halved, seeded, fruit scooped into 1-inch balls with a melon baller

1 ripe cantaloupe, halved, seeded, fruit scooped into 1-inch balls with a melon baller

$1/2$ pint fresh strawberries, hulled and quartered

$1/4$ cup sugar, or more to taste (this will depend on the sweetness of the fruit)

3 tablespoons amaretto liqueur

$1/2$ cup crumbled amaretti cookies, shortbread, or vanilla wafer cookies

1. Combine the honeydew, cantaloupe, strawberries, sugar, and amaretto in a large mixing bowl, and toss gently but thoroughly to combine. Cover with plastic wrap and let sit for 5 to 10 minutes before serving.

2. Divide the fruit among six to eight small dessert bowls, and sprinkle the crumbled cookies evenly over the top of each dessert. Serve immediately.

6 to 8 servings

FRESH BERRIES WITH BALSAMIC DRIZZLE AND ALMOND CREAM

Prep time: 10 minutes **Cook time:** 5 minutes **Total:** 15 minutes

Balsamic vinegar and fresh fruit is classic Italian fare. Here, we reduce the balsamic vinegar to bring out its sweetness, then pair it with fresh berries and a simple cream cheese blend for one knockout combination.

. . . .

½ cup balsamic vinegar

1½ cups sour cream

½ cup plus 2 tablespoons cream cheese, at room temperature

¼ cup confectioners' sugar

½ teaspoon almond extract

1 pound fresh strawberries, hulled and sliced or quartered

1 cup fresh raspberries

1 cup fresh blackberries or blueberries

3 tablespoons chopped almonds, lightly toasted

1. Pour the balsamic vinegar into a small saucepan and bring to a boil. Cook until reduced to ¼ cup (about half the original volume) and syrupy, about 3 minutes. Transfer to a small bowl and set aside to cool while you assemble the desserts.

2. In a mixing bowl, combine the sour cream, cream cheese, confectioners' sugar, and almond extract. Whisk until the sugar has dissolved and the mixture is very smooth.

3. When ready to serve the dessert, divide the berries evenly among six dessert bowls. Place a generous dollop of the sour cream mixture over the berries, and then drizzle with some of the balsamic drizzle. Garnish with the almonds, and serve immediately.

6 servings

FLAMBÉED STRAWBERRY SAUCE
FOR ANGEL FOOD CAKE OR ICE CREAM

Prep time: 10 minutes **Cook time:** 3 minutes **Total:** 13 minutes

Airy angel food cake is a perfect vehicle for this orange-scented strawberry sauce. There is a simple elegance to this dessert, and it is practically guilt-free. Serve the sauce over ice cream if you're feeling more indulgent.

2 tablespoons unsalted butter

1 pound fresh strawberries, hulled and quartered

¼ cup sugar

2 tablespoons brandy

2 tablespoons orange-flavored liqueur (such as Triple Sec, Cointreau, or Grand Marnier)

4 cups store-bought angel food cake, cut into 1-inch cubes, or 2 pints vanilla ice cream

1 cup lightly sweetened whipped cream, for serving (optional)

Fresh mint leaves, for garnish

1. Set a 12-inch sauté pan over medium-high heat and add the butter. Once the butter has melted, add the strawberries and sugar and sauté, stirring often, for 1½ to 2 minutes. Remove the pan from the heat and add the brandy and liqueur. Carefully tilt the pan toward the open flame to ignite the liquor. Once lit, swirl the pan until the flames die down, 30 to 45 seconds. Alternatively, if using an electric stove, simply reduce the sauce over high heat for 45 seconds instead of flaming it. (If serving over ice cream, you may wish to allow the sauce to cool slightly before serving.)

2. Divide the cake or ice cream evenly among four small dessert bowls. Spoon the warm strawberries over the top, and garnish with the whipped cream, if desired, and mint leaves.

4 servings

40 Minutes
OR LESS

BROCCOLI AND CHEESE SOUP

Prep time: 20 minutes **Cook time:** 15 minutes **Total:** 35 minutes

This classic combination of flavors lends itself well to this simple, creamy soup. By cooking the broccoli just right, the soup retains a vibrant bright green color. Serve this as a starter to any meal or with a sandwich or salad for a complete meal. So good for you, too.

2 tablespoons olive oil

1½ cups thinly sliced yellow onions

1 tablespoon sliced garlic

1 teaspoon salt

¼ teaspoon cayenne pepper

5 cups chicken stock or canned, low-sodium chicken broth

4 cups broccoli florets

1½ cups (6 ounces) shredded medium sharp cheddar cheese

Simple Croutons (page 136), for garnish (optional)

1. Heat the olive oil in a 6-quart stockpot over medium heat. When it is hot, add the onions, garlic, salt, and cayenne pepper. Sauté until the onions are soft and translucent, 4 to 5 minutes.

2. Add the chicken stock and bring to a boil. Once the stock is boiling, add the broccoli and cook until fork-tender, about 5 minutes.

3. Remove the soup from the heat and let it cool slightly. Then puree the soup, in batches, in a blender, adding the cheese in three additions while blending (see Note). Adjust the seasoning if necessary, garnish with croutons if desired, and serve hot.

Note: Please use caution when blending hot liquids; blend only small amounts at a time, with the blender tightly covered and a kitchen towel held over the top.

1½ quarts, 4 to 6 servings

QUICK RED BEAN SOUP

Prep time: 10 minutes **Cook time:** 26 minutes **Total:** 36 minutes

This soup is inspired by one of my favorite New Orleans classics: red beans and rice. You can easily serve a bowl of this soup garnished with some cooked white rice for a heartier meal. Oh, yeah, baby, let the New Orleans in me come out!

1 tablespoon vegetable oil

6 ounces (1 cup) smoked ham or smoked sausage, finely chopped

1½ cups chopped yellow onions

½ cup finely chopped celery

½ cup finely chopped green bell pepper

2 bay leaves

½ teaspoon cayenne pepper

2 tablespoons minced garlic

Four 15.5-ounce cans red beans, drained

6 cups chicken stock or canned, low-sodium chicken broth

2 tablespoons chopped green onions, green and white parts, for garnish

1. Heat the vegetable oil in a Dutch oven or large pot over high heat. Add the ham, onions, celery, bell pepper, bay leaves, and cayenne, and cook until the vegetables are lightly caramelized and very tender, about 6 minutes. Add the garlic and cook, stirring, for about 30 seconds. Add the red beans and chicken stock, and bring to a boil. Reduce the heat and simmer uncovered, stirring occasionally, for 10 minutes.

2. Using a potato masher, mash some of the beans slightly to thicken the broth. Continue cooking for another 10 minutes, or until the soup has thickened and the flavors have come together.

3. Remove from the heat and discard the bay leaves. Stir in the green onions, and adjust the seasoning if necessary. Serve hot.

2 generous quarts, about 8 servings

CHICKEN AND RICE SOUP

Prep time: 15 minutes **Cook time:** 25 minutes **Total:** 40 minutes

I think most of us are reminded of our childhoods when we think of chicken and rice soup. It really can hit the spot sometimes—so simple and yet so delicious. Keep in mind that if the soup is made in advance, the rice will continue to soak up the broth as it sits. Feel free to add more broth as you like.

2 pounds boneless, skinless chicken breasts, cut into 3/4-inch dice

1 tablespoon Emeril's Original Essence or Creole Seasoning (page 29)

1 tablespoon olive oil

2 cups diced onions (small dice)

1 1/2 cups diced carrots (small dice)

1 1/2 cups diced celery (small dice)

1 tablespoon minced garlic

1 teaspoon dried basil

1 teaspoon salt

1/4 teaspoon crushed red pepper

2 quarts chicken stock or canned, low-sodium chicken broth, plus more if needed

1/2 cup uncooked long-grain white rice (see Note)

One 5-ounce bag prewashed spinach

1. Place the chicken in a medium bowl, season with the Essence, and set aside.

2. Heat the olive oil in a 6-quart (or larger) soup pot over medium-high heat. Add the onions, carrots, and celery and cook, stirring occasionally, until the onions are translucent, about 5 minutes.

3. Add the garlic, basil, salt, and crushed red pepper, and continue to cook for 1 minute. Add the chicken and cook for 3 minutes. Add the broth and the rice, cover the pot, and bring to a boil over high heat. Remove the cover, reduce the heat to a simmer, and cook until the rice is just tender, about 12 minutes.

4. Stir in the spinach, and serve immediately.

Note: If you have cooked white rice on hand, omit the uncooked rice and simply stir in about 1 1/2 cups cooked rice just before you add the spinach.

3 1/2 quarts, 6 to 8 servings

CARROT GINGER SOUP

Prep time: 8 minutes **Cook time:** 22 minutes **Total:** 30 minutes

The ginger in this soup gives it a nice little kick. Though we suggest serving it hot, it can also be nice ice-cold on a hot summer day.

4 tablespoons (½ stick) butter

2 pounds carrots, cut into large dice (about 4 cups)

2 cups diced onions (medium dice)

¼ cup (about 2 ounces) peeled and sliced fresh ginger

6 sprigs fresh thyme, tied in a bundle with kitchen twine

2 teaspoons salt

¾ teaspoon freshly ground white pepper

6 cups water

Sour cream, for garnish (optional)

1. Melt the butter in a 6-quart (or larger) soup pot over high heat. Add the carrots, onions, ginger, thyme bundle, salt, and white pepper, and cook for 2 minutes. Then add the water, cover the pot, and bring to a boil. Remove the cover, reduce the heat to medium-low, and simmer for 15 minutes.

2. Remove the pot from the heat, and remove the thyme bundle. Blend the soup until it is completely smooth, using an immersion blender or in three batches in a blender (see Note).

3. Transfer the pureed soup to a 4-quart pot or other serving dish. Stir to combine, and adjust the seasoning to taste. Serve hot, garnished with a dollop of sour cream if desired.

Note: Please use caution when blending hot liquids; blend only small amounts at a time, with the blender tightly covered and a kitchen towel held over the top.

2½ quarts, about 6 servings

SPICY SMOKED SAUSAGE, TOMATO, AND MUSHROOM SOUP

Prep time: 10 minutes **Cook time:** 30 minutes **Total:** 40 minutes

Make sure to use a good-quality sausage here. My favorite would be chorizo, but it is also wonderful with andouille or other spicy smoked pork sausage. This soup is thick and hearty—a "manly-man" soup, if you will.

1 tablespoon olive oil

1 pound firm (smoked) chorizo or other spicy smoked sausage, diced or crumbled into 1/2-inch pieces

8 ounces button mushrooms, wiped clean and quartered, or diced if very large

1 1/2 cups diced onions

1/2 cup diced red bell pepper

1/2 cup diced green bell pepper

2 tablespoons thinly sliced garlic

Two 28-ounce cans whole tomatoes, roughly chopped, with juices

4 cups chicken stock or canned, low-sodium chicken broth

1/4 cup coarsely chopped fresh soft herbs (such as marjoram and/or basil)

1 1/2 teaspoons salt

3/4 teaspoon crushed red pepper

1. Heat the oil in a large nonreactive saucepan or Dutch oven over medium-high heat. When it is hot, add the sausage and cook, stirring occasionally, until it is browned around the edges, about 4 minutes.

2. Add the mushrooms, onions, bell peppers, and garlic to the pan and cook, stirring occasionally, until the vegetables are soft and lightly browned, 7 to 8 minutes.

3. Add the tomatoes and their juices, chicken stock, herbs, salt, and crushed red pepper and bring to a boil. Reduce the heat to a simmer, and cook until the flavors have married, about 15 minutes. Serve hot.

About 3 quarts, 8 to 10 servings

HOT AND SOUR SOUP

Prep time: 15 minutes Cook time: 9 minutes Total: 24 minutes

Oh, yeah, babe. Cure your cold with this one! This is a perfect balance between spicy and sour. It's an Asian classic—and it doesn't get much simpler than this. If you're a vegetarian, feel free to substitute veggie stock and cubes of tofu for the chicken broth and chicken strips. For less heat, reduce the red pepper.

8 cups chicken stock or canned, low-sodium chicken broth

6 ounces thinly sliced mushrooms (such as shiitake or button)

$1/4$ cup soy sauce

$1/4$ cup minced fresh ginger

2 tablespoons minced garlic

$3/4$ teaspoon crushed red pepper

3 tablespoons cornstarch

$1/4$ cup plus 3 tablespoons freshly squeezed lime juice

8 ounces skinless, boneless chicken breast, cut into thin strips

1 teaspoon dark Asian sesame oil

2 tablespoons thinly sliced green onion tops

1. Combine the stock, mushrooms, soy sauce, ginger, garlic, and crushed red pepper in a 4-quart pot. Cover and bring to a boil. Remove the cover, reduce the heat to a simmer, and cook until the mushrooms are tender, 7 to 8 minutes.

2. Whisk the cornstarch and the lime juice together in a small bowl. Add the cornstarch mixture and the chicken to the soup. Bring to a boil, and cook until the soup thickens, about 1 minute.

3. Stir in the sesame oil and sliced green onions, and serve hot.

About 2$1/2$ quarts, 4 to 6 servings

POTATO AND LEEK SOUP

Prep time: 10 minutes **Cook time:** 30 minutes **Total:** 40 minutes

The trick to this soup lies in not overcooking the potatoes. Cook them until they are just tender, then quickly puree them to make sure that they don't become overly starchy. Though I just love this soup served hot on a cool, crisp day, you could also serve it chilled—an especially nice option for make-ahead meals.

. . . .

1 large or 2 small leeks (about 1 pound)

2 bay leaves

20 black peppercorns

4 sprigs fresh thyme

2 tablespoons butter

2 slices bacon, diced

1/2 cup dry white wine

5 cups chicken stock or canned, low-sodium chicken broth

1 to 1 1/4 pounds russet potatoes, peeled and diced into 1-inch cubes

1 1/2 teaspoons salt

3/4 teaspoon freshly ground white pepper

1/2 to 3/4 cup crème fraîche or heavy cream

2 tablespoons snipped fresh chives

1. Trim the green portions of the leek, and using 2 of the largest and longest leaves, make a bouquet garni by folding the 2 leaves around the bay leaves, peppercorns, and thyme. Tie into a package-shaped bundle with kitchen twine, and set aside. (Alternatively, tie the 2 leek leaves, bay leaves, peppercorns, and thyme together in a piece of cheesecloth.)

2. Using a sharp knife, halve the white part of the leek lengthwise. Rinse the leek well under cold running water to rid it of any sand. Slice thinly crosswise and set aside.

3. Melt the butter in a large soup pot over medium heat, and add the bacon. Cook, stirring occasionally, until the bacon is soft and has rendered most of its fat, about 5 minutes. Add the chopped leeks and cook until wilted, about 5 minutes. Add the wine and bring to a boil. Add the reserved bouquet garni and the chicken stock, potatoes, salt, and white pepper. Bring to a boil. Then reduce the heat to a simmer and cook for about 20 minutes, or until the potatoes are tender and the soup is very flavorful.

4. Remove the bouquet garni and puree the soup using an immersion blender or in batches in a blender (see Note). Stir in the crème fraîche, and adjust the seasoning if necessary. Serve immediately, with some of the snipped chives sprinkled over the top of each bowl of soup.

Note: Please use caution when blending hot liquids; blend only small amounts at a time, with the blender tightly covered and a kitchen towel held over the top.

About 1¹/₂ quarts, 4 to 6 servings

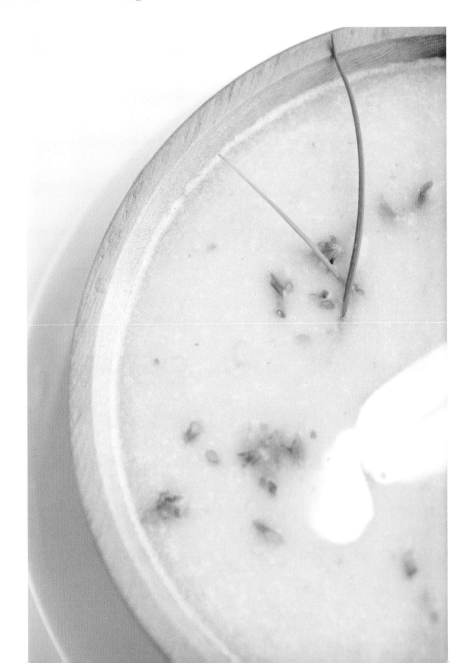

GARDEN VEGETABLE SOUP

Prep time: 12 minutes **Cook time:** 23 minutes **Total:** 35 minutes

Don't be afraid to make this straightforward, veggie-packed soup your own by using the vegetables you especially like or you have on hand. For instance, replace the zucchini and yellow squash with frozen green peas and frozen corn. If you're a tomato lover, two cups of chopped canned tomatoes can be substituted for two cups of the broth. Also, you could gild the lily by adding three cups of cooked macaroni or other small pasta, or a bit of cooked rice, right before serving. The sky's the limit here.

. . . .

6 sprigs parsley

2 bay leaves

2 tablespoons olive oil or butter

2 cups diced onions

$1^{1}/_{2}$ cups diced carrots

$1^{1}/_{2}$ cups diced celery (small dice, with or without leaves)

2 tablespoons minced garlic

8 ounces button mushrooms, wiped clean, stemmed, and quartered (about 2 cups)

4 quarts beef, chicken, or vegetable stock or canned, low-sodium beef, chicken, or vegetable broth

$1^{1}/_{2}$ teaspoons salt

$^{3}/_{4}$ teaspoon freshly ground black pepper

2 cups broccoli or cauliflower florets, cut into bite-size pieces

1 cup diced zucchini (large dice)

1 cup diced yellow squash (large dice)

One 10-ounce bag prewashed spinach

$^{1}/_{2}$ cup grated Parmigiano-Reggiano cheese (optional)

1. Tie the parsley sprigs and bay leaves together with a piece of kitchen twine. Set aside.

2. Heat the olive oil in a 6-quart (or larger) soup pot over high heat. Add the onions, carrots, celery, and the parsley bundle, and cook for 2 minutes, stirring frequently. Add the garlic and mushrooms, and cook for 3 minutes. Add the broth, salt, and pepper. Cover the pot and bring to a boil. Remove the cover, reduce the heat to medium-low, and simmer for 12 minutes.

3. Add the broccoli, zucchini, yellow squash, and spinach to the soup. Simmer for 5 minutes.

4. Remove the parsley bundle and serve the soup hot, garnished with the grated cheese if desired.

4 quarts, 6 to 8 servings

POTATO AND TURKEY HOT DOG SOUP WITH HERBS

Prep time: 15 minutes **Cook time:** 25 minutes **Total:** 40 minutes

My mom, Hilda, used to make this soup for me, my brother Mark, and my sister Dolores when we were growing up, and we ate it up like no one's business. Here I've subbed turkey hot dogs for the regular variety, but really any good-quality hot dog will do. Your kids are gonna love this one!

2 tablespoons olive oil

8 ounces turkey hot dogs, cut into
   1/2-inch-thick rounds

1 cup thinly sliced onion

1 tablespoon minced garlic

1 tablespoon chopped fresh thyme

1 1/2 teaspoons chopped fresh sage

1 1/4 to 1 1/2 pounds russet potatoes,
   peeled and diced into 1-inch
   cubes

1 quart chicken stock or canned,
   low-sodium chicken broth

1 teaspoon salt

1/2 teaspoon freshly ground black
   pepper

1 bay leaf

1 cup finely diced tomatoes

1/2 cup heavy cream

1 tablespoon chopped fresh parsley

1. Heat a 2-quart saucepan over medium-high heat and add the olive oil. When it is hot, add the hot dogs and cook, stirring occasionally, until they are caramelized on both sides, about 3 minutes. Remove the hot dogs from the pan and set them aside.

2. Add the onion and garlic to the pan and cook, stirring occasionally, until the onion is wilted and the garlic is fragrant, about 4 minutes. Add the thyme and sage and sauté for 1 minute. Add the potatoes, chicken stock, salt, pepper, and bay leaf, and bring to a boil. Reduce the heat to a simmer and cook until the potatoes are tender, about 20 minutes.

3. Remove the bay leaf, and using an immersion blender (or in batches in a blender), quickly puree the soup until smooth (see Note).

4. Return the hot dogs to the soup and add the tomatoes, heavy cream, and chopped parsley. Rewarm gently and serve hot.

Note: Please use caution when blending hot liquids; blend only small amounts at a time, with the blender tightly covered and a kitchen towel held over the top.

About 1 1/2 quarts, 4 to 6 servings

CREAM OF TOMATO SOUP

Prep time: 10 minutes **Cook time:** 24 minutes **Total:** 34 minutes

If you've never made homemade cream of tomato soup, you don't know what you're missing! This soup is the perfect accompaniment to any grilled sandwich, but I especially love it next to the Prosciutto and Mozzarella Panini on page 40. Use the balsamic vinegar to finish at the end if you like. And if you're fresh out of cream, the soup is still delicious without it. Just tell everyone, "It's simply tomato soup."

2 tablespoons olive oil

1 cup chopped onion

1/2 cup chopped carrot

1/2 cup chopped celery

1 tablespoon minced garlic

Two 28-ounce cans whole tomatoes, with juices

2 cups chicken stock or canned, low-sodium chicken broth

1 teaspoon salt

1 teaspoon freshly ground black pepper

1/2 cup heavy cream

3 tablespoons chopped mixed fresh herbs (such as marjoram and basil)

1 tablespoon balsamic vinegar (optional)

1. Set a 3-quart pot over medium-high heat. Add the olive oil, and when it is hot, add the onion, carrot, and celery. Sauté the vegetables, stirring occasionally, until the onion is translucent, 3 minutes. Add the garlic and sauté until fragrant, about 30 seconds. Add the tomatoes with their juices and the chicken stock, and bring the liquid to a boil. Reduce the heat to a simmer, season with the salt and pepper, and cook for 5 minutes.

2. Break up the tomatoes a bit with the back of a wooden spoon or spatula, and continue to cook until the soup is slightly thickened, about 15 minutes.

3. Remove the soup from the heat and puree it using an immersion blender (or in batches in a blender) until smooth (see Note). Stir in the heavy cream and the herbs, and rewarm until hot. Finish with the balsamic vinegar, if desired, and serve.

Note: Please use caution when blending hot liquids; blend only small amounts at a time, with the blender carefully covered and a kitchen towel held over the top.

About 2 quarts, 4 to 6 servings

SHRIMP AND ZUCCHINI FRITTERS WITH ROASTED RED PEPPER MAYO

Prep time: 25 minutes (including Roasted Red Pepper Mayo) **Cook time:** 15 minutes
Total: 40 minutes

What a great hors d'oeuvre or party food . . . let's serve it to the family! It's fun, easy, and delicious.

Roasted Red Pepper Mayo
(recipe follows)

2 cups all-purpose flour

1$\frac{1}{2}$ teaspoons baking powder

2 teaspoons salt

1$\frac{1}{2}$ teaspoons Emeril's Original
Essence or Creole Seasoning
(page 29), plus more if desired

$\frac{1}{4}$ teaspoon cayenne pepper

1$\frac{1}{4}$ cups milk

2 eggs

Vegetable oil, for frying

1$\frac{1}{2}$ zucchinis (about $\frac{1}{2}$ pound)

1 pound medium to large shrimp,
peeled and deveined

1 tablespoon freshly squeezed
lemon juice

1 tablespoon chopped fresh
parsley, plus more for garnish

1. Make the Roasted Red Pepper Mayo and set aside.

2. In a medium bowl, combine the flour, baking powder, 1$\frac{1}{2}$ teaspoons of the salt, $\frac{3}{4}$ teaspoon of the Essence, and the cayenne. In a small bowl, whisk together the milk and eggs. Add the liquid ingredients to the dry ingredients, and whisk until smooth. Set aside.

3. Heat 4 to 6 inches of oil to 350° F in a 6-quart pot or deep-fryer.

4. While the oil is heating, cut the zucchinis into small dice (about 2 cups), and place in a small bowl. Cut the shrimp into $\frac{1}{4}$-inch pieces and add to the bowl, along with the remaining $\frac{3}{4}$ teaspoon Essence, remaining $\frac{1}{2}$ teaspoon salt, and the lemon juice and parsley. Mix to combine. Add this mixture to the batter and stir to incorporate.

5. Using a 2-tablespoon scoop, carefully drop 10 portions of the batter into the hot oil. Cook, turning the fritters as necessary, until nicely browned on all sides, 4 to 5 minutes total. Drain on paper towels and repeat with the remaining batter.

6. Sprinkle chopped parsley over the fritters, season with additional Essence if desired, and serve immediately, with the Roasted Red Pepper Mayo alongside.

About 30 fritters

Roasted Red Pepper Mayo

$1/2$ cup diced roasted red pepper (from about $3/4$ cup packed jarred roasted red pepper)
$3/4$ cup mayonnaise
1 tablespoon minced garlic
$1/4$ teaspoon salt
$1/8$ teaspoon cayenne pepper

Combine all the ingredients in the bowl of a food processor, and process for 30 seconds. Scrape down the sides of the bowl with a rubber spatula, and process for 30 seconds longer. Store in an airtight container in the refrigerator for up to 1 week.

1$1/2$ cups

CREAMY SHRIMP AND GREEN ONION DIP

Prep time: 20 minutes **Cook time:** 10 minutes **Total:** 30 minutes

This is an exceptional dip. You probably won't even make it to the table with this one. If you plan to share, have a Plan B.

1 pound medium shrimp, peeled and deveined

2 teaspoons Emeril's Original Essence or Creole Seasoning (page 29)

1 tablespoon olive oil

8 ounces cream cheese, at room temperature

3 tablespoons mayonnaise

1/2 cup chopped green onions, white and green parts

1/3 cup minced celery

2 teaspoons freshly squeezed lemon juice

1 teaspoon finely grated lemon zest

1/2 teaspoon salt

1/2 teaspoon freshly ground white pepper

1/4 teaspoon cayenne pepper

1/4 teaspoon Worcestershire sauce

Crackers or French bread toasts, for serving

1. Combine the shrimp, Essence, and olive oil in a mixing bowl.

2. Heat a nonstick skillet over medium-high heat. When the skillet is hot, add the seasoned shrimp and cook until lightly golden and just cooked through, 3 to 4 minutes. Transfer the shrimp to a plate or shallow bowl and place in the freezer until chilled, 5 to 10 minutes.

3. While the shrimp are chilling, combine all the remaining ingredients (except the crackers) in a mixing bowl. Stir until smooth and creamy.

4. When the shrimp have chilled, remove them from the freezer and coarsely chop them. Add them to the cream cheese mixture and stir well to combine. Taste, and adjust the seasoning if necessary. Serve as is or chilled, with your favorite crackers.

Almost 3 cups, 6 to 8 servings

SEARED SHRIMP SALAD

Prep time: 17 minutes **Cook time:** 8 minutes **Total:** 25 minutes

This light and refreshing salad makes for a perfect warm-weather meal when avocados are in season.

. . . .

1/4 cup freshly squeezed orange juice

2 tablespoons freshly squeezed lime juice

1 teaspoon honey

3/4 teaspoon crushed red pepper

1/2 teaspoon soy sauce

1/2 teaspoon plus a pinch of salt

1/4 cup plus 2 tablespoons olive oil

1 pound large shrimp, peeled and deveined

One 5-ounce bag prewashed mixed greens (about 8 cups)

2 oranges, peeled and segmented (see page 19)

1/2 cup thinly sliced red onion

1 ripe avocado, halved, seeded, and thinly sliced

1. Combine the orange juice, lime juice, honey, 1/2 teaspoon of the crushed red pepper, the soy sauce, and 1/4 teaspoon of the salt in a small nonreactive bowl. Whisk to blend. In a slow, steady stream, whisk in the 1/4 cup olive oil. Set the vinaigrette aside.

2. Heat 1 tablespoon of the remaining olive oil in a 12-inch sauté pan over medium-high heat. In a bowl, toss the shrimp with the remaining 1 tablespoon olive oil, and season with 1/4 teaspoon salt and 1/4 teaspoon crushed red pepper. Add the shrimp to the pan, in two batches if necessary, and cook until they have curled and are just cooked through, 2 minutes on each side. Transfer the shrimp to a paper towel–lined plate and reserve.

3. In a large mixing bowl, combine the greens, oranges, red onion, and pinch of salt. Whisk the vinaigrette, and add 3 tablespoons to the salad. Toss lightly to combine, and then divide the salad among four serving plates. Take 3 to 4 slices of the avocado and fan them out on top of each salad. Divide the shrimp evenly among the salads. Drizzle a little more vinaigrette over the shrimp and avocado, and serve immediately.

4 servings

EMERIL'S NOODLE SALAD

Prep time: 15 minutes **Cook time:** 10 minutes **Total:** 25 minutes

Though we call for egg noodles here, feel free to use other noodles, such as soba, rice noodles, linguine, fettuccine, you name it!

Salt for the pasta water

1 pound egg noodles

1/2 cup salted peanuts

6 tablespoons soy sauce

1/4 cup rice wine vinegar

2 tablespoons dark Asian
   sesame oil

2 tablespoons honey

1 teaspoon minced fresh ginger

1 teaspoon minced garlic

1/2 teaspoon crushed red pepper

1 large seeded cucumber, cut into
   1/4-inch-thick slices (about
   4 cups)

1 1/2 cups grated carrots

1/2 cup thinly sliced green onions,
   cut on the diagonal

1. Bring a large pot of salted water to a boil. Add the noodles and cook according to the package directions until just tender. Drain the noodles in a colander, rinse them under cold running water until cool, and set aside.

2. Set an 8-inch (or smaller) skillet over low heat. Add the peanuts and toast, tossing as needed and being careful not to let them burn, until the oils begin to release and the nuts are fragrant, 2 minutes. Set aside. When they are cool enough to handle, chop the nuts.

3. In a medium bowl, whisk together the soy sauce, rice wine vinegar, sesame oil, honey, ginger, garlic, and crushed red pepper. Add the cucumber, carrots, and green onions. Add the noodles and peanuts, and mix thoroughly. Serve immediately, or refrigerate until ready to serve. (Can be stored, covered, in the refrigerator for up to 2 days.)

4 servings

GARDEN VEGETABLE SALAD

Prep time: 20 minutes **Inactive time:** 20 minutes **Total:** 40 minutes

This is a marinated salad: the vegetables are simply mixed together and tossed with the dressing. The flavors mingle in just twenty minutes! Delicious.

4 cups sliced cabbage
($1/2$-inch-wide slices)

3 cups broccoli florets, cut into bite-size pieces (about 2 small heads)

2 cups halved and sliced yellow or zucchini squash ($1/4$-inch-thick slices)

$1^1/2$ cups sliced carrots
($1/4$-inch-thick slices)

$1/2$ cup thinly sliced red onion

$1/2$ cup thinly sliced radishes

$1/4$ cup diced red bell pepper

1 teaspoon salt

$3/4$ teaspoon freshly ground black pepper

$1/4$ cup cider vinegar

1 teaspoon Dijon mustard

1 teaspoon sugar

$1/2$ cup plus 2 tablespoons vegetable oil (such as canola)

$1/4$ cup finely grated Parmigiano-Reggiano cheese

1. In a medium bowl, combine the cabbage, broccoli, squash, carrots, red onion, radishes, and red bell pepper. Season with $3/4$ teaspoon of the salt and $1/2$ teaspoon of the black pepper, and mix well. Set aside.

2. In a small bowl, whisk together the vinegar, mustard, sugar, remaining $1/4$ teaspoon salt, and remaining $1/4$ teaspoon pepper. While constantly whisking, add the oil in a thin, steady stream until completely incorporated. Stir in the cheese.

3. Pour the dressing over the vegetables and mix thoroughly. Cover with plastic wrap and refrigerate for at least 20 minutes, or as long as overnight, before serving.

4 to 6 servings

SIMPLE CROUTONS

Prep time: 5 minutes **Cook time:** 30 minutes **Total:** 35 minutes

I like to make a big batch of croutons when I find myself with a day-old baguette and a little time, and then store them in airtight containers so that I have them on hand for whenever I need them. They will keep this way for a couple of weeks—as long as you make sure to cook them until they're totally crisp and golden. My kids love snacking on them, and they really add such a nice crunch and texture to so many dishes.

1 French baguette (about
    12 ounces), preferably day-old,
    cut into 1/2-inch dice

1/2 cup extra-virgin olive oil

3/4 teaspoon Emeril's Original
    Essence or Creole Seasoning
    (page 29)

1/8 teaspoon salt

1/8 teaspoon freshly ground black
    pepper

1. Preheat the oven to 300°F.

2. Combine all of the ingredients in a large mixing bowl, and toss quickly to coat the croutons well. Transfer the croutons to a baking sheet and spread them out in a single layer. Bake, rotating the baking sheet front to back midway through, until crisp all the way through and golden, 25 to 30 minutes. Remove from the oven and set aside to cool completely. Store in an airtight container at room temperature.

About 6 cups

CHICKPEA SALAD WITH TABBOULEH

Prep time: 25 minutes **Total:** 25 minutes

The addition of bulgur wheat to this simple chickpea salad makes for an unexpectedly delicious combination. Who would've thought? Oh, yeah, babe—good and good for you, too!

. . . .

$\frac{1}{2}$ cup bulgur wheat

1 cup hot water

$\frac{1}{2}$ cup chopped green onions, white and green parts

$\frac{1}{4}$ cup chopped fresh parsley

$\frac{1}{4}$ cup chopped fresh mint

$\frac{1}{4}$ cup diced oil-packed sun-dried tomatoes

$\frac{1}{4}$ cup plus 2 tablespoons freshly squeezed lemon juice

2 teaspoons minced garlic

1 teaspoon fine sea salt

$\frac{3}{4}$ teaspoon crushed red pepper

$\frac{3}{4}$ cup extra-virgin olive oil

$\frac{1}{2}$ cup (about 4 ounces) crumbled feta cheese

Two 14-ounce cans chickpeas, rinsed and drained

1. Place the bulgur in a mixing bowl, add the hot water, and set aside to soak for 25 minutes.

2. While the bulgur is soaking, prep the remaining ingredients. Combine the green onions, parsley, mint, sun-dried tomatoes, lemon juice, garlic, sea salt, and crushed red pepper in a medium bowl. Gradually whisk in the olive oil.

3. Drain the bulgur, squeezing it to remove any excess liquid, and add it to the herb-tomato mixture. Fold in the feta cheese and chickpeas. Taste, and adjust the seasoning if necessary. Serve at room temperature or chilled.

4 servings

CHICKEN QUESO BURGERS

Prep time: 12 minutes Cook time: 28 minutes Total: 40 minutes

I know you love burgers and cheese, and this chicken version is super-cheesy. Because of the generous amount of cheese, be sure to use a nonstick skillet. The griddled onions make the burger extra-special. After this, you're sure to be making them for all your sandwiches.

2 eggs, lightly beaten

8 ounces cheddar cheese, grated (about 2 cups)

One 4-ounce can (about $^1/_3$ cup) minced green chiles, drained

2 tablespoons chopped fresh oregano

3 teaspoons chili powder

1 teaspoon ground cumin

2$^1/_2$ teaspoons salt

2 pounds ground chicken thigh meat

$^3/_4$ cup fine unseasoned dry breadcrumbs

1$^1/_2$ cups minced onions

1 cup olive oil

8 hamburger buns

Lettuce, tomato, and mayonnaise, for garnishing burgers (optional)

1. In a large bowl, combine the eggs, cheese, chiles, oregano, 1$^1/_2$ teaspoons of the chili powder, the cumin, and 2 teaspoons of the salt. Add the ground chicken and the breadcrumbs, and mix until well blended. Divide the mixture into 8 portions, and shape each portion into a 1-inch-thick patty. Lay the patties on a tray, cover with plastic wrap, and refrigerate until ready to cook.

2. Combine the onions, $^3/_4$ cup of the olive oil, remaining 1$^1/_2$ teaspoons chili powder, and remaining $^1/_2$ teaspoon salt in a small bowl. Divide the onion mixture evenly among the cut sides of the hamburger buns, and spread it out with a brush to coat.

3. Heat a 12-inch nonstick skillet over medium-high heat. In batches, toast the buns, coated sides down, in the skillet until the onions cook slightly and stick to the buns and the bread is lightly toasted, 2 to 3 minutes. Set the buns aside and wipe the skillet clean.

4. In the same nonstick skillet, heat 2 tablespoons of the remaining olive oil over medium heat. Add 4 patties and cook until an instant-read thermometer registers 165°F when inserted into the center of a patty, about 4 minutes per side. Set the patties aside; keep warm. Repeat with the remaining 2 tablespoons olive oil and 4 patties. Place the patties between the toasted buns and serve immediately, with lettuce, tomato, and mayonnaise, if desired.

8 servings

CHILI-RUBBED SHRIMP WRAPS

Prep time: 20 minutes **Cook time:** 8 minutes **Total:** 28 minutes

These shrimp marinate for just ten minutes. For a twist, skewer and grill them instead of sautéing. They can be served as part of an hors d'oeuvre tray, in a salad, with pasta tossed in olive oil, salt, and pepper, or as we've outlined here, in a tortilla.

8 tablespoons olive oil

1/4 cup plus 1 tablespoon freshly squeezed lime juice

3 tablespoons chopped fresh cilantro

4 teaspoons minced garlic

1 teaspoon Mexican chili powder

1 1/2 pounds large shrimp, peeled and deveined

1/2 cup sour cream

3/4 teaspoon salt

Four 14-inch flour tortillas

8 ounces red-leaf lettuce, rinsed, spun dry, and cut into 1-inch pieces

1 medium tomato, diced

1 Hass avocado, halved, seeded, and thinly sliced

1/2 cup grated Monterey Jack or pepper Jack cheese

1. In a medium bowl, combine 6 tablespoons of the olive oil, the 1/4 cup lime juice, 2 tablespoons of the cilantro, the garlic, and 1/2 teaspoon of the chili powder. Add the shrimp and set aside to marinate at room temperature for 10 minutes, turning them every few minutes.

2. In a small bowl, combine the sour cream, the remaining 1 tablespoon lime juice, the remaining 1 tablespoon cilantro, 1/4 teaspoon of the remaining chili powder, and 1/4 teaspoon of the salt. Stir well and set aside.

3. Heat the remaining 2 tablespoons olive oil in a 12-inch sauté pan over medium-high heat. Remove the shrimp from the marinade and season with the remaining 1/2 teaspoon salt and 1/4 teaspoon chili powder. In two batches, cook the shrimp for 2 minutes per side. Remove from the pan and allow to cool slightly before assembling the sandwiches.

4. Lay the tortillas on a clean work surface. Arrange one-fourth of the shrimp across the lower third of each tortilla, leaving about 2 inches of space on either side. Divide the lettuce, tomato, avocado slices, and grated cheese evenly among the tortillas, scattering them over the shrimp. Then drizzle some of the dressing over each. Fold both sides of each tortilla in toward the center, then roll the lower edge of the tortilla up, burrito-style, forming a wrap. Position the wraps on a serving plate, seam side down, and slice each in half on the diagonal. Serve immediately, or refrigerate and serve within 1 hour.

4 servings

SPICY PORK WRAPS
WITH CREAMY COLESLAW

Prep time: 10 to 14 minutes **Cook time:** 16 minutes **Total:** 26 to 30 minutes

No marinade needed. The tenderloins are coated in an intensely spiced rub, seared, sliced, and cloaked in a cool, creamy slaw. These babies pack a punch! Who's makin' this sandwich?

2 tablespoons light brown sugar

1 tablespoon chili powder

2 teaspoons dry mustard

2 teaspoons salt

$3/4$ teaspoon dried oregano

$3/4$ teaspoon cayenne pepper

2 pork tenderloins (about 1 pound each), tail ends tucked under and tied

2 tablespoons olive oil

Six 10-inch flour tortillas

One 14-ounce bag coleslaw mix, or 14 ounces shredded mixed cabbage and carrots

$1/3$ cup buttermilk

$1/4$ cup mayonnaise

$1/4$ cup minced green onions, white and green parts

1. Preheat the oven to 400°F.

2. Combine the brown sugar, chili powder, dry mustard, $1^{1}/_{2}$ teaspoons of the salt, the oregano, and $1/2$ teaspoon of the cayenne in a small bowl. Generously rub the mixture all over the pork tenderloins.

3. Heat the olive oil in a 12-inch sauté pan over medium-high heat. Add the tenderloins and sear, turning frequently, until evenly crusted on all sides (they will be dark in color because of the sugar), 2 to 4 minutes. Transfer the pork to a baking sheet and roast in the oven for 12 minutes, or until the internal temperature registers 145°F on an instant-read thermometer inserted into the center.

4. Remove the tenderloins from the oven, transfer them to a cutting board, and tent with foil. Let rest for at least 10 minutes before slicing. While the pork is resting, wrap the tortillas in aluminum foil and place them in the oven until warmed through, 6 to 8 minutes.

5. Make the coleslaw by combining the coleslaw mix with the buttermilk, mayonnaise, green onions, remaining $1/2$ teaspoon salt, and remaining $1/4$ teaspoon cayenne pepper. Toss well to combine, and set aside until ready to serve.

6. To assemble the pork wraps, slice the pork tenderloin in thin slices at an angle. Place ¼ cup of the coleslaw on the lower half of each tortilla, leaving about 2 inches on either side, and then divide the pork slices evenly among the tortillas. Fold in both sides of the tortillas, and then roll the tortillas up, burrito-style. Slice in half and serve immediately.

4 to 6 servings

CHICKEN PATTY POCKETS
WITH MINTED YOGURT SAUCE

Prep time: 19 minutes **Cook time:** 7 minutes **Total:** 26 minutes

You don't need a giant roasting spit for mouthwatering meat. You're on the Emeril Express here. Fill pita pockets with lettuce, tomatoes, and alfalfa sprouts for good measure, add your spicy baked chicken patties, and dollop with the Minted Yogurt Sauce.

1 pound ground chicken thigh meat

2 large egg whites, lightly beaten

1/2 cup fine unseasoned dry breadcrumbs

1/4 cup finely chopped onion

1/4 cup chopped fresh parsley

1 tablespoon minced garlic

1 teaspoon salt

1/2 teaspoon cayenne pepper

1/2 teaspoon ground coriander

1/4 teaspoon ground nutmeg

1/4 teaspoon ground cumin

2 tablespoons olive oil

Pita bread, for serving

Lettuce, sliced tomatoes, and alfalfa sprouts, for garnishing sandwiches (optional)

Minted Yogurt Sauce, for serving (optional; recipe follows)

1. Position a rack as close as possible to the broiler element and preheat the broiler.

2. In a large bowl, combine the chicken, egg whites, breadcrumbs, onion, parsley, garlic, salt, and spices. Mix until well blended, using a large spoon. Line a rimmed baking sheet with aluminum foil, and drizzle with 1 tablespoon of the olive oil. Divide the seasoned meat into 8 portions, 2½ to 3 ounces each, and place them on the prepared baking sheet. Shape each into an oval patty and flatten it slightly. Brush or drizzle the remaining 1 tablespoon olive oil over the patties.

3. Broil until lightly browned, about 7 minutes, or until an instant-read thermometer registers 165°F when inserted into the center of a patty. Serve on pita bread, with lettuce, tomatoes, sprouts, and Minted Yogurt Sauce, if desired.

4 servings

Minted Yogurt Sauce

Prep time: 10 minutes **Total:** 10 minutes

1 cup plain yogurt

1/2 cucumber, peeled, seeded, and cut into small dice (about 1 cup)

2 tablespoons chopped fresh mint
1 tablespoon freshly squeezed lime juice
¾ teaspoon salt
¼ teaspoon ground cumin
¼ teaspoon sweet paprika
⅛ teaspoon cayenne pepper
Pinch of sugar

1. Place the yogurt in a fine-mesh strainer set over a bowl, and let it drain for 3 minutes while you assemble the other ingredients. Discard any liquid that drains from the yogurt.

2. Combine the cucumber, mint, lime juice, salt, cumin, paprika, cayenne, and sugar in a small bowl. Stir to blend.

3. Add the drained yogurt and stir to combine. Serve immediately, or refrigerate, covered, for up to 1 hour to allow the flavors to come together before serving.

About 2 cups

OVEN-CRISPY FRENCH FRIES WITH PAPRIKA-PARMESAN SALT

Prep time: 10 minutes **Cook time:** 30 minutes **Total:** 40 minutes

These fries are not just for burgers. While they're in the oven, make the Crispy Pan-Roasted Chicken with Garlic-Thyme Butter (page 193), the Steak au Poivre (page 86), the Classic Moules Marinière (page 79), or the Broiled Salmon with a Warm Tomato-Lemon Vinaigrette (page 72)! Do I need to keep going? Ahhhh, you get it!

2 large baking potatoes (about 1½ pounds), scrubbed well

¼ cup olive oil

1 tablespoon Emeril's Original Essence or Creole Seasoning (page 29)

¾ teaspoon salt

¼ cup finely grated Parmigiano-Reggiano cheese

1 tablespoon sweet paprika

½ teaspoon garlic powder

¼ teaspoon onion powder

1. Preheat the oven to 425°F.

2. Pat the potatoes dry and cut them lengthwise into ½-inch-thick slices. Turn each side flat and slice again lengthwise into even ½-inch-thick fries. Place the potatoes in a mixing bowl and add the olive oil, Essence, and ¼ teaspoon of the salt. Toss well to combine. Then transfer the fries to a large baking sheet and arrange them in one even layer so that they are not touching. Roast, scraping the potatoes from the baking sheet with a metal spatula and turning them over halfway through, until golden brown and crispy, 30 minutes.

3. While the potatoes are cooking, combine the cheese, paprika, garlic powder, onion powder, and the remaining ½ teaspoon salt in a small bowl and stir to blend.

4. When the potatoes are crisp and brown, remove them from the oven and transfer to a serving platter. Sprinkle the potatoes with the Paprika-Parmesan Salt, and serve hot.

4 to 6 servings

ORZO "RISOTTO" WITH TOMATO, MOZZARELLA, AND BASIL

Prep time: 10 minutes **Cook time:** 20 minutes **Total:** 30 minutes

Here you'll find orzo cooked in the style of risotto. This works equally well as a quick and easy side dish or as a vegetarian entrée when served with a nice salad or grilled veggies.

3 tablespoons olive oil

1/3 cup minced red onion

1 tablespoon minced garlic

2 cups orzo pasta

4 cups chicken stock, or canned, low-sodium chicken broth, heated

1 teaspoon salt

1/2 teaspoon freshly ground black pepper

2 cups diced fresh tomatoes

1/2 cup diced fresh mozzarella cheese

1 1/2 tablespoons thinly sliced basil

1. Heat the olive oil in a medium saucepan over medium heat. When it is hot, add the red onion and garlic and cook until fragrant, about 30 seconds. Add the orzo and stir well to coat.

2. Gradually add the hot chicken stock in 1/2-cup increments, stirring until all of the stock has been absorbed before adding more, until the stock is completely incorporated and the pasta is just tender, 14 to 16 minutes. Season with the salt and pepper.

3. Add the tomatoes to the orzo and cook until they are just heated through, 1 to 2 minutes. Add the mozzarella and cook for another 2 to 3 minutes, or just until it is incorporated.

4. To serve, spoon the risotto into bowls and garnish with the basil.

4 servings

SHIITAKES AND BACON WITH PENNE

Prep time: 15 minutes **Cook time:** 17 minutes **Total:** 32 minutes

Talk about tasty—this dish is a real winner. The combination of shiitake mushrooms and bacon really works here, trust me. If you're a pancetta-lover like me, feel free to substitute about 4 ounces of diced pancetta for the bacon. *Mama mia!*

1 pound penne pasta

4 slices thick-cut bacon, cut into
  1/2-inch pieces

7 ounces shiitake mushrooms,
  wiped clean, stemmed, and
  thinly sliced

1 1/2 cups diced onions (small dice)

2 teaspoons minced garlic

Two 14.5-ounce cans diced
  tomatoes, with juices

1/4 cup chopped fresh basil

1 1/2 teaspoons salt, plus more for
  the pasta water

1 teaspoon freshly ground black
  pepper

1/4 cup extra-virgin olive oil

Grated Parmigiano-Reggiano
  cheese, for garnish (optional)

1. Bring a large pot of salted water to a boil. Add the penne and cook until just tender, about 11 minutes. Drain the pasta in a colander.

2. While the pasta is cooking, heat a 12-inch (or larger) sauté pan over medium-high heat. Add the bacon and cook, stirring occasionally, until crisp, 5 to 6 minutes. Add the mushrooms and onions and cook until the mushrooms are browned and the onions are soft, 5 to 6 minutes. Add the garlic and cook until fragrant, about 30 seconds.

3. Add the drained pasta to the pan, along with the tomatoes, basil, salt, pepper, and olive oil. Cook, tossing often, until the pasta is thoroughly combined and heated through, about 5 minutes.

4. Serve immediately, garnished with grated cheese if desired.

4 to 6 servings

PENNE WITH SAUSAGE AND ESCAROLE

Prep time: 12 minutes **Cook time:** 20 minutes **Total:** 32 minutes

Those of you who don't love escarole had better try it again . . . the sweetness of the Italian sausage here really complements its flavor beautifully. A simple pasta dish for any day of the week.

1 pound penne pasta

1 teaspoon olive oil

2 medium onions, cut into small dice (about 2 cups)

1 red bell pepper, cut into medium dice (about 1 cup)

$^1/_2$ teaspoon salt, plus more for the pasta water

$^1/_2$ teaspoon freshly ground black pepper

$1^1/_2$ pounds sweet Italian sausage, casings removed (or bulk sausage)

2 teaspoons minced garlic

1 bunch escarole or mustard greens, rinsed, stemmed, and torn into bite-size pieces (about 8 cups)

$^1/_2$ cup grated Parmigiano-Reggiano cheese

$^1/_4$ teaspoon crushed red pepper

2 tablespoons extra-virgin olive oil

1. Bring a large pot of salted water to a boil. Add the penne and cook until just tender, about 11 minutes. Drain the pasta in a colander, reserving 1 cup of the cooking water, and set aside.

2. While the water is heating and the pasta is cooking, heat the olive oil in a 14-inch sauté pan over medium heat. Add the onions, bell pepper, $^1/_2$ teaspoon salt, and black pepper, and cook until the vegetables are soft, about 4 minutes. Add the sausage and cook, breaking the pieces up with the back of a wooden spoon, until browned, 6 to 8 minutes. Add the garlic and escarole, and cook for 5 minutes longer.

3. Add the cooked pasta and the reserved cooking water, and stir gently to combine. Simmer just until everything is heated through, about 2 minutes.

4. Transfer the mixture to a large serving bowl. Add the cheese and crushed red pepper, and toss to combine. Drizzle with the extra-virgin olive oil, and serve immediately.

6 to 8 servings

SPAGHETTI WITH CARAMELIZED ONIONS AND ANCHOVIES

Prep time: 10 minutes **Cook time:** 25 minutes **Total:** 35 minutes

The amount of anchovies in this recipe may seem alarming, but, yes, two whole tins is correct here, and makes for a deliciously sweet and salty pasta sauce. Oh, this dish brings me back to the south of Italy in a heartbeat.

1 pound spaghetti

1/3 cup olive oil

2 tablespoons unsalted butter

8 cups thinly sliced onions

2 tablespoons thinly sliced garlic

Two 2-ounce cans flat anchovy fillets (packed in olive oil, not salt), well drained

1 1/2 teaspoons kosher salt, plus more for the pasta water

1 teaspoon freshly ground black pepper

2 tablespoons chopped fresh parsley

1/2 cup extra-virgin olive oil

1. Bring a large pot of salted water to a boil. Add the spaghetti and cook until just tender, about 9 minutes. Drain the pasta in a colander, reserving 1 cup of the cooking water, and set aside.

2. While the water is heating and the pasta is cooking, set a 14-inch sauté pan over medium-high heat and add the olive oil and butter. Once the butter melts, add the onions and cook, stirring occasionally with a heat-resistant rubber spatula, until they have softened and caramelized, about 20 minutes. (Should the onions get too dry and begin sticking in spots before they are all caramelized, add a bit of water, stir, and continue cooking.)

3. Add the garlic and anchovies to the pan and cook, stirring, until fragrant, 2 to 3 minutes.

4. Add the drained pasta and the reserved pasta water to the pan and season with the 1 1/2 teaspoons salt and the pepper. Cook, tossing to combine, until the pasta is heated through and the water has nearly evaporated, 3 to 4 minutes. Remove from the heat, add the parsley, and drizzle with the extra-virgin olive oil. Toss to combine, and serve immediately.

Note: It is not necessary to chop the anchovies; they will break into small pieces while cooking.

4 to 6 servings

THREE-CHEESE BAKED MACARONI

Prep time: 8 minutes Cook time: 20 minutes Inactive time: 10 minutes Total: 38 minutes

This super-easy custard-style macaroni has the perfect blend of cheeses and bacony goodness for any mac-n-cheese lover.

8 ounces elbow macaroni

3 ounces bacon (about 3 strips), sliced crosswise into $1/2$-inch pieces

$1\frac{1}{2}$ teaspoons minced garlic

3 eggs

$1\frac{1}{2}$ cups evaporated milk

$1/2$ teaspoon salt, plus more for the pasta water

$1/4$ teaspoon cayenne pepper

$1/8$ teaspoon freshly grated nutmeg

6 ounces sharp cheddar cheese, grated (about $1\frac{1}{2}$ cups)

2 ounces Monterey Jack cheese, grated (about $1/2$ cup)

1 ounce Parmigiano-Reggiano cheese, finely grated (about $1/2$ cup)

1. Preheat the oven to 425°F.

2. Bring a large pot of salted water to a boil. Add the macaroni and cook until just tender, about 6 minutes. Drain, and set aside.

3. While the pasta is cooking, heat a small sauté pan over medium heat and add the bacon. Cook until the fat is rendered and the bacon is crisp, about 6 minutes. Add the garlic and cook until fragrant, 30 seconds to 1 minute. Drain the fat from the bacon-garlic mixture, and transfer the mixture to a medium bowl.

4. Add the drained macaroni to the bacon mixture, and stir to combine.

5. In a large bowl, whisk the eggs and evaporated milk together. Add the $1/2$ teaspoon salt, cayenne, nutmeg, and grated cheeses, and mix well. Add the macaroni-bacon mixture, and stir well to blend.

6. Transfer the macaroni to an 8- or 9-inch square baking dish or gratin dish of similar size. Using a spoon, gently spread the mixture to form an even layer. Place in the oven and bake for 12 minutes. Remove the macaroni and cheese from the oven and let it rest for at least 10 minutes before serving.

4 to 6 servings

SHRIMP AND LINGUINE FRA DIAVOLO

Prep time: 15 minutes **Cook time:** 12 minutes **Total:** 27 minutes

This is hot as the devil! The classic Fra Diavolo preparation uses lobster, but here I've simplified it a bit for the home cook with sweet shrimp, preferably from the Gulf of Mexico. Talk about making me smile!

· ·

1 pound linguine

6 tablespoons extra-virgin olive oil

1 cup chopped onion

3 tablespoons minced garlic

2 to 3 teaspoons crushed red pepper, to taste

1½ cups tomato sauce

2 tablespoons tomato paste

1½ pounds shrimp, peeled and deveined

1 teaspoon salt, plus more for the pasta water

2 tablespoons chopped fresh parsley

½ cup grated Parmigiano-Reggiano cheese (optional)

1. Bring a large pot of salted water to a boil. Add the linguine and cook until barely tender, about 8 minutes. Drain, reserving 1 cup of the cooking water, and set aside.

2. While the pasta is cooking, set a 14-inch sauté pan over medium-high heat and add the olive oil. Once the oil is hot, add the onion and cook until lightly caramelized and wilted, 3 to 4 minutes. Add the garlic and sauté until fragrant, about 30 seconds. Add the crushed red pepper and sauté briefly; then add the tomato sauce and tomato paste. Cook until the sauce has reduced by about half, about 3 minutes. Add the shrimp to the sauce and cook for 2 minutes.

3. Add the pasta and the reserved cooking water to the pan, and cook until the pasta is heated through and coated with the sauce, 3 minutes. Season the pasta with the salt, and garnish with the parsley. Toss to combine, and serve with the grated cheese if desired.

6 servings

PENNE ALLA PUTTANESCA

Prep time: 15 minutes **Cook time:** 25 minutes **Total:** 40 minutes

Puttanesca sauce is nothing more than the combination of tomatoes, onion, garlic, basil, anchovies, and capers—ingredients typically kept on hand in most Italian households and one of my favorite sauces of all time. Make a big batch of this and freeze it in small containers so you can pull some out for a quick and easy meal anytime.

. . . .

Salt

1/4 cup extra-virgin olive oil, plus more for serving

1 large onion, chopped

1/2 teaspoon crushed red pepper

8 cloves garlic, minced

One 28-ounce can Italian plum tomatoes, roughly chopped or broken into pieces, with juices

1 cup halved pitted Kalamata olives, drained

1/4 cup nonpareil capers, drained, liquid reserved separately

5 canned anchovy fillets, or to taste, finely chopped

1/2 teaspoon dried basil, crushed between your fingers

Freshly ground black pepper

1 pound penne rigate pasta

Finely grated Parmigiano-Reggiano cheese, for serving (optional)

1. Bring a large pot of salted water to a boil.

2. While the water is heating, heat the oil in a large nonreactive saucepan or skillet over medium-high heat. Add the onion and crushed red pepper, and sauté until the onion is tender and beginning to caramelize, about 4 minutes. Add the garlic and cook for 1 minute, stirring. Add the tomatoes, olives, capers, anchovies, and basil, and bring the sauce to a boil. Reduce the heat to low and simmer, uncovered and stirring occasionally, until the sauce has thickened, 15 to 20 minutes.

3. Meanwhile, cook the pasta in the boiling water until just tender, about 11 minutes. Drain the pasta, reserving the pot it was cooked in. Set the pasta aside.

4. Remove the sauce from the heat, and season it with salt and pepper to taste. Add 1 to 2 teaspoons of the reserved caper juice, to taste.

5. Return the penne to the pasta pot over medium-high heat. Add half of the pasta sauce and cook, stirring, until heated through, about 2 minutes. Serve hot, with more sauce ladled on top of each serving if desired, drizzled with additional extra-virgin olive oil. Garnish with grated cheese, if desired.

4 to 6 servings

BEEF STROGANOFF WITH EGG NOODLES

Prep time: 15 minutes **Cook time:** 25 minutes **Total:** 40 minutes

Now this is what real beef and mushrooms taste like! Splurge on 1½ pounds of good rib-eye steak and feed six. The beef is quickly sautéed. The sauce is full of browned mushroom goodness. Put them together and add your noodles. *Whoa!*

. . . .

8 ounces extra-wide egg noodles

1½ pounds rib-eye steak, sliced into ½-inch-thick strips

2 teaspoons salt, plus more for the pasta water

1 teaspoon freshly ground black pepper

4 tablespoons olive oil

3 tablespoons butter

1½ cups thinly sliced onions

12 ounces button mushrooms, wiped clean, stemmed, and sliced (about 4 cups)

1 tablespoon chopped garlic

1 tablespoon all-purpose flour

2 cups beef stock or canned, low-sodium beef broth

½ cup sour cream

1 tablespoon chopped fresh parsley

1. Bring a large pot of salted water to a boil. Add the noodles and cook until just tender, about 8 minutes.

2. While the noodles are cooking, season the beef with 1 teaspoon of the salt and ½ teaspoon of the pepper.

3. Heat 2 tablespoons of the olive oil in a 12-inch sauté pan over high heat. In two batches, brown the beef strips for 1 to 2 minutes per side. Transfer the beef to a plate and set aside.

4. Add the butter to the sauté pan, and when it has melted, add the onions. Reduce the heat to medium and cook until the onions are soft, about 4 minutes. Add the mushrooms and continue to cook, stirring as needed, until nicely browned, about 7 minutes.

5. When the noodles are cooked, drain them, transfer them to a bowl, and toss with the remaining 2 tablespoons olive oil. Cover to keep warm until ready to add to the sauce.

6. Add the garlic and the remaining 1 teaspoon salt and ½ teaspoon pepper to the mushroom mixture and cook, stirring, for 1 minute. Sprinkle with the flour, and stir. Increase the heat to high and whisk in the broth. When the liquid comes to a boil, reduce the heat to a simmer and cook for 5 minutes.

7. Return the beef, and any juices that have accumulated on the plate, to the sauté pan. Whisk in the sour cream and parsley, and remove the pan from the heat. Fold in the warm noodles, and serve immediately.

6 servings

PASTA PRIMAVERA

Prep time: 15 minutes **Cook time:** 15 minutes **Total:** 30 minutes

This colorful sauce is a simpler, lighter version of the primavera sauce most often encountered. Feel free to substitute other veggies, as desired. As you will see, this makes a very large batch of pasta, enough for six to eight healthy appetites.

1 pound rotini or penne pasta

5 tablespoons butter

2 cups chopped red onions

1 cup chopped red bell pepper

2 teaspoons salt, plus more for the pasta water

1 teaspoon freshly ground black pepper

$1\frac{1}{2}$ tablespoons minced garlic

1 pound zucchini or yellow squash (or a mixture of both), halved lengthwise and cut crosswise into $\frac{1}{2}$-inch half-moon pieces (about 4 cups)

2 cups frozen mixed peas and carrots

1 cup diced canned tomatoes, with juices

$\frac{1}{2}$ cup finely grated Parmigiano-Reggiano cheese, plus more for serving

$\frac{1}{2}$ cup thinly sliced basil (optional)

$\frac{1}{3}$ cup extra-virgin olive oil

1. Bring a large pot of salted water to a boil. Add the rotini and cook until just tender, about 11 minutes. Drain, reserving $\frac{3}{4}$ cup of the cooking water, and set aside.

2. While the pasta is cooking, melt the butter in a 14-inch sauté pan over medium-high heat. Add the onions and bell pepper and cook until soft, 4 minutes. Add the 2 teaspoons salt, black pepper, and garlic, and cook for 1 minute longer. Add the squash and continue to cook, stirring as needed, for 2 minutes. Add the peas and carrots and cook for 2 minutes. Add the tomatoes and continue to cook, stirring, for 2 minutes.

3. Add the pasta and the reserved cooking water to the sauce and cook until the pasta is heated through and the ingredients are well combined, 1 to 2 minutes. Remove from the heat and fold in the Parmigiano-Reggiano and basil, if desired. Then drizzle with the extra-virgin olive oil. Garnish with more cheese, if desired, and serve hot.

6 to 8 servings

GREEN ONION RICE PILAF

Prep time: 10 minutes **Cook time:** 20 minutes **Total:** 30 minutes

This simple rice dish goes well with so many things, it's not even funny. The method is foolproof. All you need is a timer to keep you from worrying about the rice while it's cooking, leaving you free to tend to other things . . .

¼ cup olive oil

½ cup chopped onion

1 teaspoon minced garlic

2 cups long-grain white rice

2 teaspoons salt

1 teaspoon freshly ground white pepper

3 cups chicken stock or canned, low-sodium chicken broth or water

¼ cup thinly sliced green onion tops

1. Place a 2-quart ovenproof saucepan over medium-high heat and add the olive oil. Once the oil is hot, add the onion and cook, stirring often, until translucent and beginning to soften, about 4 minutes. Add the garlic and sauté for 30 seconds. Add the rice and sauté, stirring, until fragrant, 3 to 4 minutes. Season the rice with the salt and white pepper.

2. Add the chicken stock to the pan and cook, stirring occasionally, until the water comes to a boil. Then cover the pan, reduce the heat to low, and cook for 20 minutes.

3. Remove the pan from the heat and let the rice stand, covered, for 5 minutes. Remove the lid, add the green onion, and toss with a fork to combine.

6 cups, 6 to 8 servings

BASIC RISOTTO

Prep time: 5 minutes **Cook time:** 25 minutes **Total:** 30 minutes

Think while stirring, "Buttery, cheesy, and creamy . . . ," "Buttery, cheesy, and creamy . . . ," "Buttery, cheesy, and creamy . . ." Aah, *finito*.

¼ cup olive oil

¼ cup finely chopped shallots

2 cups Arborio rice

1 teaspoon salt

¼ teaspoon freshly ground white pepper

½ cup dry white wine

6 cups chicken stock, or canned, low-sodium chicken broth, heated

1 tablespoon butter

½ cup finely grated Parmigiano-Reggiano cheese

1 tablespoon fresh thyme leaves

1. Heat the olive oil in a 14-inch sauté pan over medium-high heat. Add the shallots and cook, stirring with a heat-resistant rubber spatula, until fragrant and soft, about 1 minute. Add the rice and cook until the grains are opaque, about 2 minutes. Then add the salt, white pepper, and white wine. Continue cooking, stirring the rice as needed, until nearly all the liquid has been absorbed.

2. Reduce the heat to medium, stir in ¾ cup of the hot broth, simmer, and stir until nearly all the liquid has been absorbed. Continue in this manner, adding the broth in ¾-cup increments and only adding more once the previous addition has been absorbed, until all the broth has been used and the risotto is tender and creamy, about 20 minutes.

3. Fold in the butter, cheese, and thyme. Remove from the heat, adjust the seasoning if necessary, and serve immediately.

4 servings

BLACK BEAN CAKES

Prep time: 16 minutes **Cook time:** 8 minutes **Total:** 24 minutes

Talk about "knock your socks off"! These bean cakes end up crispy and crusty on the outside, but oh so tender and creamy on the inside. A true study in contrasts, this dish is elevated to notches unknown when served garnished with your favorite guacamole, salsa, and sour cream.

. . . .

7 tablespoons olive oil

1 small onion (5 to 6 ounces), cut into small dice

2 teaspoons minced garlic

$\frac{1}{2}$ cup all-purpose flour

2 tablespoons Emeril's Original Essence or Creole Seasoning (page 29)

Two 15.5-ounce cans black beans, drained and quickly rinsed

2 tablespoons chopped fresh cilantro, plus more for garnish

1 egg, lightly beaten

$\frac{1}{2}$ teaspoon salt, plus more to taste

$\frac{1}{2}$ teaspoon freshly ground black pepper

$\frac{1}{2}$ teaspoon ground cumin

$\frac{1}{2}$ teaspoon ground coriander

2 teaspoons hot sauce

1. Heat 1 tablespoon of the olive oil in a medium sauté pan over medium heat. When it is hot, add the onion and cook until soft and lightly caramelized, about 3 minutes. Add the garlic and cook until fragrant, about 30 seconds. Remove from the heat and set aside to cool.

2. Place the flour in a shallow bowl or plate, and stir in the Essence. Set aside.

3. In a medium mixing bowl, mash the black beans well with the back of a fork—the mixture should be relatively smooth, with no whole beans remaining. Stir in the cooled onion mixture, cilantro, egg, salt, pepper, cumin, coriander, and hot sauce and mix well. Divide the mixture into 8 evenly sized patties (about $\frac{1}{3}$ cup each).

4. Heat the remaining 6 tablespoons olive oil in a medium nonstick skillet over medium heat. When the oil is hot, dust the patties in the seasoned flour mixture and carefully transfer them to the hot skillet (the cakes will be delicate). Cook the cakes until golden brown on both sides and heated through, about 2 minutes per side.

5. If necessary, season with more salt. Garnish with chopped cilantro, and serve immediately.

4 servings

TURKEY AND PINTO BEAN TOSTADAS

Prep time: 10 minutes **Cook time:** 25 minutes **Total:** 35 minutes

For this open-face taco we crisp the tortillas in the oven. Hold on to your sombreros—you're in for a real treat.

....

4 tablespoons olive oil

1 medium onion, chopped

1 pound ground turkey (preferably 85/15 blend)

2 tablespoons Mexican chili powder

1½ tablespoons chopped garlic

1½ teaspoons ground cumin

1 teaspoon salt

Two 15-ounce cans pinto beans, drained and briefly rinsed

1½ cups chicken stock or canned, low-sodium chicken broth

15 fresh cilantro sprigs, stems and leaves chopped separately

8 to 10 corn tortillas

Condiments as desired for serving (such as grated cheese, chopped tomato, chopped red onion, shaved lettuce, salsa, pickled jalapeños, sour cream)

1. Preheat the oven to 400°F.

2. Set a skillet over medium-high heat, add 2 tablespoons of the olive oil and the onion, and cook, stirring, for 2 minutes. Add the turkey, chili powder, garlic, cumin, and salt, and cook, stirring and breaking up the meat as it browns, for 5 minutes. Add the beans, chicken stock, and chopped cilantro stems, and bring to a boil. Cook, mashing the beans frequently against the bottom and sides of the skillet, until the mixture is thickened to a refried bean consistency and the flavors have come together, about 15 minutes.

3. While the turkey-bean mixture is simmering, brush the tortillas on both sides with the remaining 2 tablespoons olive oil. Place them on baking sheets and bake in the oven until crisp, 12 to 15 minutes. Remove from the oven, and transfer to paper towels to drain and crisp briefly before serving.

4. Stir the cilantro leaves into the turkey-bean mixture. Spread the mixture over the crisped tortillas, and garnish with condiments as desired.

8 to 10 tostadas, 4 to 6 servings

CREAMY WHITE BEANS WITH SAUSAGE

Prep time: 5 minutes **Cook time:** 25 minutes **Total:** 30 minutes

This creamy bean dish can work well as either an appetizer or a main course, and is delicious when eaten with pieces of crusty French bread. Don't forget to drizzle it with the best extra-virgin olive oil you have on hand, Italian-style, as this small gesture really makes a big difference.

3 tablespoons olive oil

1 tablespoon minced garlic

12 ounces hot smoked sausage, sliced into ½-inch-thick rounds

One 14.5-ounce can diced tomatoes, with juices

Five 15-ounce cans cannellini beans, rinsed and drained

1 tablespoon chopped fresh rosemary

1 teaspoon chopped fresh thyme

3 cups fresh spinach or arugula, rinsed and spun dry

Salt and freshly ground black pepper

Extra-virgin olive oil, for serving

Crusty French or peasant bread, warmed, for serving (optional)

1. Heat the oil in a large heavy Dutch oven over medium heat. Add the garlic and sauté until fragrant, about 30 seconds. Add the sausage and tomatoes. Increase the heat to medium-high and simmer for 2 minutes. Add the beans and bring to a boil. Then reduce the heat to a simmer and cook until the beans are tender and flavorful, about 20 minutes.

2. Remove the pot from the heat and stir in the rosemary, thyme, and spinach. Season with salt and pepper to taste, and serve hot in wide shallow bowls, drizzled with extra-virgin olive oil. Pass the French bread, if desired.

2 quarts, 4 to 6 servings

BACON BRAISED GREEN BEANS

Prep time: 8 minutes Cook time: 17 minutes Total: 25 minutes

This modern take on the Southern classic will leave you wanting more! Since this version is quick-cooked, the beans stay crisp-tender—but oh, they're coated with sautéed onions and little pieces of bacon. Don't make me talk about it!

1 tablespoon olive oil

6 slices bacon, diced

1 cup thinly sliced onion

2 tablespoons sliced garlic

2 pounds green beans, rinsed, ends trimmed

1 cup chicken stock or canned, low-sodium chicken broth or water

1 teaspoon salt

1/2 teaspoon freshly ground black pepper

1. Set a Dutch oven over medium heat, and add the olive oil. Once the oil is hot, add the bacon and cook, stirring occasionally, until it is well browned, about 5 minutes. Add the onion and garlic and cook, stirring occasionally, until the onion is translucent, 3 to 4 minutes. Add the green beans and toss to combine with the bacon and onion.

2. Increase the heat to medium-high and add the chicken stock. As soon as the stock begins to boil, place the lid on the pan and cook the beans for about 6 minutes. Remove the lid, season the beans with the salt and pepper, and toss well. Replace the lid and cook until the beans are tender, 1 or 2 minutes longer.

3. Remove from the heat and transfer the beans to a serving dish or small platter to serve.

4 to 6 servings

CREAMED MUSTARD GREENS

Prep time: 16 minutes **Cook time:** 23 minutes **Total:** 39 minutes

Everyone loves creamed spinach, but check out this version of the dish made with mustard greens and you'll be an instant convert. We have also made this with turnip greens and kale with good success—truthfully, any type of green will do, and each type adds its own unique flavor. To stay within the forty-minute time frame, make sure you start the sauce while the greens are cooking.

Salt

6 pounds mustard greens, rinsed well, tough stems and ribs removed

3 tablespoons canola oil

1 cup finely chopped onion

2 large cloves garlic, minced

1 cup half-and-half

8 ounces Neufchâtel cheese, cut into pieces

Pinch of freshly grated nutmeg

Kosher salt and freshly ground black pepper

1. Bring a large stockpot of salted water to a boil. Prepare a large bowl of ice water. Add half of the mustard greens to the boiling water, a little at a time, pushing them down into the water. Let the water return to a boil and then cook until tender, about 10 minutes. Using tongs, transfer the greens to the bowl of ice water. Repeat with the remaining greens. Drain the greens very well and squeeze them dry in a kitchen towel. Finely chop, and set aside. (If your stockpot is large enough, you may be able to do this in one batch and save yourself some time.)

2. While the greens are cooking, heat the canola oil in a 12-inch skillet over medium heat. Add the onion and garlic, and cook until softened, about 6 minutes. Stir in the half-and-half and the Neufchâtel, and simmer, stirring occasionally, until thickened and creamy, about 3 minutes.

3. Add the greens to the cream mixture and cook, stirring, until warmed through, about 3 minutes. Season with the nutmeg, add salt and pepper to taste, and serve.

6 cups, 4 to 6 servings

SAUTÉED MUSHROOMS WITH FRESH THYME

Prep time: 15 minutes **Cook time:** 20 minutes **Total:** 35 minutes

This mushroom dish is the perfect accompaniment to the New York Strip with Beurre Maître d'Hôtel on page 88!

2 tablespoons olive oil

2 tablespoons unsalted butter

2 pounds button mushrooms, wiped clean, stemmed, quartered

1 cup chopped yellow onion

1 tablespoon thinly sliced garlic

1½ teaspoons fresh thyme leaves

1½ teaspoons salt

½ teaspoon freshly ground black pepper

¾ cup chicken stock or canned, low-sodium chicken broth

2 tablespoons Worcestershire sauce

1. Heat a 12-inch cast-iron skillet (or other heavy skillet) over medium-high heat, and add the olive oil. When the oil is hot, add the butter, and once it has melted, add the mushrooms, onion, garlic, thyme, salt, and pepper. Cook, stirring occasionally, until most of the liquid has been released from the mushrooms and has evaporated, about 15 minutes.

2. Add the chicken stock and cook until nearly evaporated, about 4 minutes. Add the Worcestershire sauce and cook, stirring, for 1 minute. Remove from the heat and serve immediately.

4 to 6 servings

SESAME EGGPLANT

Prep time: 11 minutes **Cook time:** 12 minutes **Total:** 23 minutes

I'm a huge eggplant fan, and love it just about any way you can imagine. Here is a quick and easy preparation that I make for the family on weeknights. Note: If you have a large enough pan, you can cook this dish in one batch and in half the time.

$\frac{1}{2}$ cup peanut oil

2 pounds eggplant, cut into $\frac{3}{4}$-inch dice

$1\frac{1}{2}$ teaspoons salt

4 green onions, bottoms minced and tops sliced, reserved separately

2 tablespoons minced garlic

$\frac{1}{2}$ teaspoon freshly ground black pepper

$\frac{1}{2}$ teaspoon crushed red pepper

1 tablespoon sesame seeds

1 tablespoon dark Asian sesame oil

1. Heat $\frac{1}{4}$ cup of the oil in a large nonstick sauté pan. When it is hot, add half of the eggplant and $\frac{3}{4}$ teaspoon of the salt. Cook until the eggplant is nicely browned and softened, stirring as necessary to promote even browning, about 5 minutes. Add half of the green onion bottoms, 1 tablespoon of the garlic, $\frac{1}{4}$ teaspoon of the black pepper, $\frac{1}{4}$ teaspoon of the crushed red pepper, $\frac{1}{2}$ tablespoon of the sesame seeds, and $\frac{1}{2}$ tablespoon of the sesame oil. Toss to combine. Transfer to a plate and set aside.

2. Repeat with the remaining ingredients.

3. Combine both batches in the same pan, add the green onion tops, and heat briefly until warmed through, 1 minute. Serve immediately.

4 servings

SPICY BRAISED GREENS

Prep time: 10 minutes **Cook time:** 20 minutes **Total:** 30 minutes

Would you like some *amazing*-tasting greens? This is the recipe! Make this once, and the next time you'll do it twice! To make this even faster, use the prewashed greens from your favorite produce section.

3 tablespoons olive oil

4 ounces smoked bacon slices, cut into 1-inch pieces (use turkey bacon if you prefer)

1 cup sliced yellow onion

1 tablespoon minced garlic

2 pounds collard greens, mustard greens, beet greens, Swiss chard, or a combination, ribs removed, chopped into bite-size pieces, and rinsed

$1/2$ teaspoon crushed red pepper, or more to taste

1 cup chicken stock or canned, low-sodium chicken broth

2 tablespoons butter

$1/4$ teaspoon salt, or more to taste

1. Heat a 12-inch sauté pan over medium-high heat and add the olive oil. When it is hot, add the bacon and cook, stirring often, until it is well browned, about 4 minutes. Add the onion and cook, stirring often, until softened, about 3 minutes. Add the garlic and cook for 30 seconds. Add the greens and cook, stirring frequently, until softened, 3 minutes.

2. Add the crushed red pepper and the chicken stock, and bring the liquid to a boil. Cover the pan and reduce the heat to medium-low. Cook until the greens are tender, about 10 minutes.

3. Remove the lid, increase the heat, and bring the liquid to a high simmer. Cook for 5 minutes or until the liquid has reduced by half. Stir in the butter, and season with the salt. Serve hot.

4 servings

BUTTERMILK MASHED POTATOES

Prep time: 10 minutes **Cook time:** 30 minutes **Total:** 40 minutes

This basic recipe is perfect as is, but feel free to embellish it with other ingredients such as goat cheese, grated cheddar cheese, roasted garlic, or sliced green onions. You just can't make the Simple Turkey Meatloaf on page 251 without making a batch of these to serve alongside!

2 pounds Yukon gold potatoes, peeled and diced into 1-inch cubes

Salt

8 tablespoons (1 stick) butter, cubed

1½ cups buttermilk

Freshly ground white pepper

1. Place the potatoes in a pot of salted water and bring to a boil. Reduce the heat to a simmer and cook until the potatoes are fork-tender, 12 to 15 minutes.

2. Remove the pot from the heat and drain the potatoes. Return the potatoes to the pot and set it over medium heat. Stir the potatoes constantly for 2 to 3 minutes to remove any excess liquid.

3. Add the butter to the potatoes and using a hand-held masher, mash the butter into the potatoes. Gradually add the buttermilk, mashing until the desired texture is achieved. Season the potatoes with salt and white pepper to taste, and serve.

6 to 8 servings

INDIAN-INSPIRED SHRIMP WITH COCONUT, CHILES, AND TOMATOES

Prep time: 23 minutes **Cook time:** 15 minutes **Total:** 38 minutes

This dish is chock-full of complex flavors that'll make your guests think that you worked for hours in the kitchen. Who needs to know otherwise? Serve it with basmati rice for an authentic taste of India.

2 tablespoons butter

2 teaspoons mustard seeds

2 teaspoons cumin seeds

1 cup finely chopped red onion

4 green serrano or jalapeño chiles, seeded and finely chopped

2 tablespoons minced fresh ginger

1 tablespoon minced garlic

One 14.5-ounce can diced tomatoes, with juices

One 13.5-ounce can unsweetened coconut milk

$1\frac{1}{2}$ pounds medium shrimp, peeled and deveined

2 teaspoons salt

2 tablespoons chopped fresh cilantro

2 tablespoons chopped fresh chives (optional)

Steamed basmati rice, for serving

1. Melt the butter in a 14-inch sauté pan over medium-high heat. Add the mustard seeds and cumin seeds and toast until fragrant, about 1 minute. Add the onion, chiles, ginger, and garlic and sauté, stirring occasionally, until the onion is translucent, about 3 minutes. Add the diced tomatoes and their juices, and cook until the liquid is reduced by half, 3 to 4 minutes. Raise the heat to high and add the coconut milk. Simmer until the milk is reduced by half, 3 to 4 minutes.

2. Season the shrimp with $1\frac{1}{2}$ teaspoons of the salt. Add the shrimp to the pan and cook, stirring as needed, until they are curled, pink, and just cooked through, about 3 minutes.

3. Remove the pan from the heat. Season with the remaining $\frac{1}{2}$ teaspoon salt, and garnish with the cilantro and chives, if desired. Serve immediately over steamed basmati rice.

4 to 6 servings

FISH EN PAPILLOTE

Prep time: 25 minutes **Cook time:** 12 minutes **Total:** 37 minutes

A meal in a pouch! It doesn't get much simpler than this!

. . . .

1½ cups thinly sliced red cabbage

1 large onion (about 12 ounces), thinly sliced

4 parsnips (about 12 ounces), cut into ⅛-inch-thick rounds

¼ cup chopped mixed soft herbs (such as parsley and tarragon)

1½ teaspoons salt

¾ teaspoon freshly ground white pepper

3 tablespoons freshly squeezed lemon juice

1 teaspoon honey

6 tablespoons olive oil

Four 6-ounce skinless fish fillets (such as red snapper or striped bass)

1. Preheat the oven to 375°F.

2. Place the cabbage, onion, parsnips, herbs, ¼ teaspoon of the salt, and ⅛ teaspoon of the white pepper in a mixing bowl and toss to combine; set aside.

3. In a small mixing bowl, whisk together the lemon juice and honey. While whisking, add the olive oil in a slow, steady stream. Season with ¼ teaspoon of the salt and ⅛ teaspoon of the white pepper. Set aside.

4. Using a paper towel, pat the fish fillets to dry them. Season each fillet on both sides with the remaining 1 teaspoon salt and ½ teaspoon white pepper.

5. Assemble the packets: Fold four 14-inch squares of aluminum foil in half, forming four rectangles. Open the rectangles, and divide the cabbage mixture evenly among them, placing it just to one side of the fold. Stir the lemon-oil mixture well, and drizzle 1 tablespoon over each portion of cabbage. Place a fish fillet on top of each, and drizzle another tablespoon over each fillet. Fold the other side of the foil over the ingredients, and then fold the edges inward two or three times to form an airtight packet that is sealed on all sides.

6. Place the packets on a baking sheet, and bake until the packets are puffed and the fish is cooked through and flakes easily when touched with a fork, about 12

minutes (the cook time may vary slightly, depending on the thickness of the fillets).

7. Remove the baking sheet from the oven, and open the packets carefully (there will be a lot of steam escaping from the packet). Serve immediately.

4 servings

SWORDFISH WITH PUTTANESCA RELISH

Prep time: 15 minutes **Cook time:** 10 minutes **Total:** 25 minutes

Unlike puttanesca pasta sauce, this is more of a relish that is basically uncooked, save for a quick warming when you're finishing the swordfish steaks in the sauté pan. The recipe uses only half of the relish that is made here; any unused puttanesca relish can be enjoyed over cooked chicken breasts, grilled fish, with pasta, or even as a topping for crostini or bruschetta. The leftover relish will keep in an airtight nonreactive container in the fridge for up to 3 days.

One and a half 14-ounce cans petite diced tomatoes, with juices

3/4 cup halved pitted Kalamata olives

1 1/2 tablespoons extra-virgin olive oil

1 tablespoon red wine vinegar

2 teaspoons minced garlic

2 teaspoons anchovy paste or finely chopped canned anchovy fillets

2 tablespoons nonpareil capers, drained

4 tablespoons chopped fresh basil

1 teaspoon freshly ground black pepper

Four 6-ounce swordfish steaks, about 1 1/2 inches thick, patted dry

1/2 teaspoon salt

2 tablespoons olive oil

1. Combine the tomatoes and their juices with the olives, extra-virgin olive oil, vinegar, garlic, anchovy paste, capers, 2 tablespoons of the basil, and 1/2 teaspoon of the black pepper in a medium bowl and set aside.

2. Season the swordfish steaks with the salt and the remaining 1/2 teaspoon black pepper. Heat the olive oil in a 12-inch sauté pan over medium-high heat. Add the swordfish and cook for 4 minutes. Turn the steaks over and cook for an additional 4 minutes.

3. Add 2 cups of the puttanesca relish to the fish and cook for 2 minutes. Transfer the fish to a serving platter or individual plates, and spoon the warm puttanesca relish over it. Garnish with the remaining 2 tablespoons basil, and more relish if desired.

4 servings, 4 cups puttanesca relish

ROASTED SCROD WITH HERBED BREADCRUMBS

Prep time: 18 minutes **Cook time:** 12 minutes **Total:** 30 minutes

Scrod, cod, baby cod, haddock—any of these fish would work beautifully in this simple preparation, which reminds me of my New England upbringing. If you're feeling indulgent, try drizzling the fillets with extra olive oil or melted butter just before serving.

Nonstick cooking spray

3 tablespoons unsalted butter

3 tablespoons minced shallot

1/2 cup fine unseasoned dry breadcrumbs

1 1/2 teaspoons salt

1/2 teaspoon freshly ground black pepper

1/4 teaspoon grated lemon zest

2 teaspoons chopped fresh parsley

2 teaspoons chopped fresh chives

2 teaspoons chopped fresh thyme

2 tablespoons olive oil

Four 6- to 8-ounce skinless young cod, scrod, or haddock fillets

1. Preheat the oven to 400°F. Lightly grease a baking sheet with nonstick cooking spray.

2. Melt the butter in a small saucepan over medium-high heat. Add the shallot and sauté until tender, 1 to 2 minutes. Transfer the shallot and butter to a medium bowl, and set aside to cool briefly.

3. Once the shallot-butter mixture has cooled slightly, add the breadcrumbs, 1/2 teaspoon of the salt, 1/4 teaspoon of the pepper, and the lemon zest, parsley, chives, and thyme. Stir to blend. Drizzle the olive oil into the breadcrumb mixture, tossing until the mixture is moistened.

4. Pat the fillets dry with a paper towel, and season with the remaining 1 teaspoon salt and 1/4 teaspoon pepper. Place the fish on the prepared baking sheet. Top each fillet evenly with the breadcrumb mixture. Place the baking sheet in the oven and bake until the crust is golden brown and the fillets are just cooked through, 10 to 12 minutes, depending on their thickness.

4 servings

SHRIMP AND FETA, GREEK-STYLE

Prep time: 5 minutes **Cook time:** 25 to 30 minutes **Total:** 30 to 35 minutes

The test kitchen made a big splash in our office the day this dish was prepared. Folks were coming out of the woodwork like crazy! Now, I must warn you: this is a bold dish that makes no apologies. If you are sensitive to spicy foods, I would suggest using less crushed red pepper than is called for here. And do not forget the crusty bread, as it's an absolutely essential part of this dish. It's just what's needed for sopping up the delicious pan juices.

½ cup plus 3 tablespoons extra-virgin olive oil

2 tablespoons minced garlic

Two 14.5-ounce cans petite diced tomatoes, with juices

½ cup clam juice

2½ teaspoons chopped fresh oregano

1 teaspoon crushed red pepper

¼ cup nonpareil capers, drained

Salt and freshly ground black pepper

2 pounds large shrimp, peeled and deveined

½ cup Pernod

8 ounces Greek feta, crumbled

1 loaf peasant bread, for serving

1. Preheat the oven to 450°F.

2. Heat the ½ cup olive oil in a large saucepan over medium-high heat. When it is hot, add the garlic and cook until fragrant, about 1 minute. Add the tomatoes and their juices, clam juice, oregano, crushed red pepper, and capers, and cook until the sauce has thickened slightly, 4 to 6 minutes. Season to taste with salt and pepper.

3. While the tomato sauce is cooking, heat the remaining 3 tablespoons olive oil in a large sauté pan. When the oil is hot, add the shrimp and cook until they are just pink on both sides, about 2 minutes. Remove the pan from the heat, and add the Pernod. Return the pan to the heat and shake it carefully to ignite the alcohol. When the flames have died down, season the shrimp lightly with salt and pepper. Do not overcook; the shrimp should not be cooked through at this point.

4. Spoon the tomato sauce into a large casserole or individual gratin dishes. Nestle the shrimp down in the sauce, and crumble the feta evenly over the top.

Bake for 10 to 12 minutes, or until the shrimp are just cooked through and the sauce is bubbly.

5. Remove from the oven and serve immediately, with pieces of crusty bread for dipping.

Note: If using an electric burner, simmer the Pernod in the pan over medium-high heat for 30 seconds.

6 servings

SALMON WITH ORANGE BUTTER SAUCE

Prep time: 8 minutes **Cook time:** 22 minutes **Total:** 30 minutes

The sauce for this simply sautéed salmon is reminiscent of some of the serious sauces found in French cuisine but don't be fooled—the dish can be on the table in no time flat.

....

¾ cup freshly squeezed orange juice

One ½-inch strip of orange zest

¼ cup julienned shallots

½ bay leaf

1 teaspoon whole black peppercorns

1 clove garlic, smashed

1 sprig fresh thyme

⅓ cup dry white wine

½ cup heavy cream

8 ounces (2 sticks) cold unsalted butter, cut into small pieces

Salt and freshly ground black pepper

Four 6-ounce salmon fillets, skin on

2 tablespoons canola or vegetable oil

1. Combine the orange juice, strip of orange zest, shallots, bay leaf, peppercorns, garlic, thyme, and wine in a saucepan, and bring to a boil. Reduce the heat to a simmer and cook until the liquid has reduced by three-fourths, about 8 minutes. Add the heavy cream and cook until the liquid has reduced by half, about 4 minutes longer. Whisk in the cold butter little by little, whisking until the sauce is smooth and thick and all the butter is incorporated, 3 to 4 minutes; do not allow the sauce to boil. Strain the sauce through a fine-mesh sieve into another saucepan, pressing on the solids to extract all the liquid; discard the solids. Season the sauce with salt and pepper to taste, and keep warm until ready to serve. (Do not allow the sauce to boil or it will separate.)

2. Season the salmon on both sides with ½ teaspoon salt and ¼ teaspoon black pepper. Heat the canola oil in a large skillet over medium-high heat. Add the salmon, skin side down, and cook until lightly browned and crisp, 3 to 4 minutes. Flip the salmon over and cook until the fish is just cooked through, about 2 minutes.

3. Serve the salmon, skin side up, immediately, with the orange butter sauce spooned around the fillets.

4 servings

BAKED FLOUNDER WITH CARROTS, SPINACH, AND AN ASIAN VINAIGRETTE

Prep time: 18 minutes **Cook time:** 12 minutes **Total:** 30 minutes

My wife, Alden, loves fish and this is one of the ways we enjoy fresh fillets at home with the family. So easy, it's just about foolproof—as long as you take care not to overcook the fish. It's also important to use the freshest fish you can find. If flounder is unavailable or too pricey, feel free to substitute any mild, white-fleshed fish fillets, but note that if you use thick fillets, the cook time will vary accordingly.

6 tablespoons extra-virgin olive oil

2 tablespoons freshly squeezed lemon juice

2 tablespoons soy sauce

2 teaspoons dark Asian sesame oil

2 teaspoons honey

1 teaspoon minced fresh ginger

1 teaspoon minced garlic

2$\frac{1}{4}$ teaspoons salt

1$\frac{1}{4}$ teaspoons freshly ground white pepper

8 ounces prewashed baby spinach, stemmed, and roughly chopped

2 carrots, sliced into ribbons with a vegetable peeler

$\frac{1}{3}$ cup mixed fresh parsley, cilantro, and tarragon leaves

Four 6-ounce skinless flounder fillets

1. Preheat the oven to 375°F.

2. In a medium bowl, combine the extra-virgin olive oil, lemon juice, soy sauce, sesame oil, honey, ginger, and garlic, and whisk well to combine. Season with $\frac{1}{4}$ teaspoon of the salt and $\frac{1}{4}$ teaspoon of the white pepper.

3. In a separate bowl, combine the spinach, carrots, and herbs, and drizzle with 6 tablespoons of the vinaigrette; toss well to combine. Arrange the salad in a glass or ceramic casserole or baking dish. Season the flounder on both sides with the remaining 2 teaspoons salt and 1 teaspoon pepper. Lay the fish over the salad, and drizzle 1 tablespoon of the vinaigrette over each of the fillets. Place in the oven and bake until the vegetables are wilted and the fish flakes easily when pierced with a fork, about 12 minutes.

4. Remove from the oven and serve the fish with some of the wilted vegetables.

4 servings

BOURSIN CHEESE, SPINACH, AND PECAN-STUFFED CHICKEN BREASTS

Prep time: 26 minutes **Cook time:** 14 minutes **Total:** 40 minutes

Everybody loves stuffed chicken breasts, so make 'em happy. If you don't have a piping bag, fill a heavy resealable plastic storage bag with the filling, snip a corner to create a diagonal opening, and squeeze.

. . . .

3 tablespoons butter

4 ounces prewashed fresh spinach

8 ounces pecans, toasted and chopped (about 1 cup)

One 5.2-ounce Black Pepper Boursin cheese (or other flavor Boursin)

Six 6- to 8-ounce boneless, skinless chicken breasts

1½ teaspoons salt

½ teaspoon freshly ground black pepper

½ cup all-purpose flour

3 teaspoons Emeril's Original Essence or Creole Seasoning (page 29)

½ cup milk

1 egg

1 cup unseasoned dry breadcrumbs

2 tablespoons olive oil

1. Preheat the oven to 400°F. Line a baking sheet with parchment paper, and set it aside.

2. Melt 1 tablespoon of the butter in a small sauté pan over medium heat. Add the spinach and cook until wilted, about 2 minutes. Remove the spinach from the pan, drain all the liquid, and chop the spinach. Transfer it to a small bowl. Add the chopped pecans and the Boursin to the spinach, and stir to combine. Using a rubber spatula, transfer the mixture to a piping bag fitted with a medium tip. Set aside.

3. Lay the chicken breasts flat on a clean work surface. With a paring knife, cut a long slit in the thick side of each breast, slicing about three-fourths of the way down and 2 inches deep to form a deep pocket (be careful not to go through the other side). Stuff each breast with the filling by piping it in tightly. Secure the opening with a toothpick. Season the breasts on both sides with ½ teaspoon of the salt and the black pepper.

4. Combine the flour and 1 teaspoon of the Essence in a shallow baking dish or bowl. In a second shallow pan, combine the milk, egg, and 1 teaspoon of the Essence. In a third shallow pan, combine the breadcrumbs, remaining 1 teaspoon Essence, and remaining 1 teaspoon salt. Dredge each chicken breast first in the flour, then in the egg wash, and lastly in the bread-crumbs; set aside.

5. Heat the olive oil and the remaining 2 tablespoons butter in a large skillet over medium-high heat. Add the chicken and sauté until browned, 2 minutes on each side. Place the seared chicken breasts on the pre-pared baking sheet, place it in the oven, and bake un-til cooked through and the temperature registers 165°F on an instant-read thermometer, about 10 min-utes.

6. Remove the toothpicks before serving.

6 servings

HONEY-LEMON-THYME CORNISH GAME HENS

Prep time: 15 minutes Cook time: 25 minutes Total: 40 minutes

What would this book be without a Cornish hen recipe? Gotta have one! Cornish hens are tiny enough for everybody to have their own, easily served. Having guests? Perfect.

Four 1-pound Cornish game hens

8 tablespoons (1 stick) butter

1 tablespoon plus 1 teaspoon chopped fresh thyme

Grated zest of 2 lemons

4 teaspoons salt

1 teaspoon freshly ground black pepper

2 tablespoons freshly squeezed lemon juice

1/3 cup honey

1 tablespoon plus 1 teaspoon soy sauce

1. Position a rack in the center of the oven and preheat the oven to 500°F. Line a large baking dish with aluminum foil, and set it aside.

2. Rinse the hens well, inside and out, under cool running water. Pat them dry with paper towels.

3. Combine 4 tablespoons of the butter, the thyme, and the lemon zest in a small bowl and use a fork to blend well. Divide the mixture into 4 portions, and spread one portion under the skin covering the breast of each hen. Combine 1 teaspoon of the salt with 1/2 teaspoon of the black pepper, and season the cavities of the hens. Truss the hens, fold the wing tips back and tuck them under, and arrange the hens breast side up in the prepared baking dish.

4. Combine the lemon juice, honey, soy sauce, and the remaining 4 tablespoons butter in a small saucepan, and warm over low heat until heated through. Divide the honey mixture in half, and set aside one portion. Use some of the remaining portion to baste the tops of the hens well. Season the hens with the remaining 3 teaspoons salt and 1/2 teaspoon pepper.

5. Transfer the baking dish to the oven and cook, basting the hens with the honey mixture about every 5 minutes, until they are nicely browned, 20 to 25 minutes. If necessary, tent the hens with foil during the last few minutes of cooking to prevent over-browning.

6. When the hens reach an internal temperature of 165°F, remove the dish from the oven and let them rest for about 5 minutes. Discard the honey mixture used for basting. Use the reserved honey mixture to drizzle over the hens before serving.

Note: To check the temperature, insert an instant-read thermometer in the thickest part of the breast, avoiding any bones.

4 servings

OVEN-ROASTED CHICKEN WINGS

Prep time: 15 minutes **Cook time:** 20 minutes **Total:** 35 minutes

If you don't want to bother with cutting the chicken wings yourself (though it only takes 5 minutes), buy little drumettes from your grocer instead. Add a little lemon juice, some herbs and spices, and roast in a smokin' hot oven. You won't have to clean the fryer or hide from your doctor. Need I say more?

4 pounds chicken wings, wing tips removed and discarded, separated at the joint

1/4 cup freshly squeezed lemon juice

1 tablespoon freshly ground black pepper

1 tablespoon garlic powder

1 tablespoon onion powder

2 teaspoons salt

2 teaspoons dried thyme

1/2 teaspoon cayenne pepper

4 tablespoons (1/2 stick) butter, melted

Your favorite sauce (such as barbecue sauce, ranch dressing, or blue cheese dressing), for serving (optional)

1. Preheat the oven to 500°F. Line a large rimmed baking sheet with aluminum foil.

2. In a large mixing bowl, combine the wings and the lemon juice and mix thoroughly. Add the pepper, garlic powder, onion powder, and salt. While crushing it between your fingers, add the thyme. Mix again, and add the cayenne and melted butter. Mix thoroughly a final time. Then transfer the wings to the prepared baking sheet, and arrange them in one layer.

3. Roast in the oven for 10 minutes. Rotate the pan and roast for 10 minutes longer, until the wings are nicely browned and cooked through. Serve as is or with your favorite dipping sauce.

4 to 6 servings

CRISPY PAN-ROASTED CHICKEN WITH GARLIC-THYME BUTTER

Prep time: 5 minutes **Cook time:** 23 to 25 minutes **Total:** 28 to 30 minutes

One whole chicken, cut in half, cooks in half the time! Go figure. You will not believe how something so simple can be so *good*. I mean, isn't it just chicken? Prepare to swoon.

One 3½-pound chicken, halved, with the breastbone, backbone, and first two digits (tips) of the wings removed

1 tablespoon kosher salt

1½ teaspoons freshly ground white pepper

4 teaspoons olive oil

2 tablespoons unsalted butter, at room temperature

1 teaspoon minced garlic

1 teaspoon fresh thyme leaves

1. Preheat the oven to 400°F.

2. Season the chicken halves on both sides with the salt and white pepper. Set a 12-inch cast-iron skillet over high heat, and when it is hot, add the olive oil. Swirl the skillet to coat it evenly, and then lay the seasoned chicken halves, skin side down, in the skillet. Sear until golden, about 3 minutes.

3. Transfer the skillet to the oven and roast until the chicken is nearly cooked through and the skin is crispy, about 17 minutes. Turn the chicken over and continue to roast, skin side up, until it is cooked through, 3 to 5 minutes.

4. While the chicken is roasting, combine the butter with the garlic and thyme in a small bowl, and stir well to blend.

5. As soon as the chicken is removed from the oven, spread the garlic butter over the skin and serve immediately.

2 to 4 servings

CHICKEN CORDON BLEU

Prep time: 25 minutes **Cook time:** 10 minutes **Total:** 35 minutes

To make things even easier, these babies can be filled and breaded up to a day ahead of time and cooked later—just six minutes in the pan and four minutes in the oven! You just wait for them to get hot and melty in the center.

Four 6-ounce boneless, skinless chicken breasts (about 1½ pounds)

½ teaspoon salt

¼ teaspoon freshly ground black pepper

6 ounces sliced Swiss cheese (4 to 6 slices)

4 ounces thinly sliced prosciutto or Black Forest ham

1 cup all-purpose flour

2 eggs

2 tablespoons milk

1 cup fine unseasoned dry breadcrumbs

1 tablespoon plus 2 teaspoons Emeril's Original Essence or Creole Seasoning (page 29)

3 tablespoons olive oil

1. Butterfly each chicken breast; then cut down the middle to separate the halves so that you have a total of 8 pieces of chicken. Place the chicken between two pieces of plastic wrap, and pound each piece, using a mallet or the bottom of a heavy skillet, to a thickness of about ¼ inch. Lay the 8 chicken pieces on a baking sheet, and sprinkle each side with the salt and pepper. Divide the cheese evenly among 4 of the chicken pieces. Arrange the prosciutto slices evenly over the cheese. Top each "filled" piece of chicken with one of the "unfilled" pieces, trying to tuck in any of the cheese or prosciutto that extends over the edges. Secure the chicken pieces together using toothpicks along both long edges.

2. Preheat the oven to 400°F, and line a baking sheet with parchment paper.

3. Place the flour in a shallow bowl. In another shallow pan, combine the eggs and milk with a fork. Place the breadcrumbs in a third shallow pan. Season the flour with 1 tablespoon of the Essence. Season the breadcrumbs with the remaining 2 teaspoons Essence. Dip each chicken scallop "sandwich" in the flour, and shake to remove any excess. Then dip it in the egg-milk mixture, and finally dip it in the seasoned breadcrumbs. Set the breaded chicken pieces on a plate.

4. Heat the olive oil in a 14-inch sauté pan over medium-high heat. Arrange all 4 chicken "sandwiches" in the pan and cook until nicely browned on one side, about 4 minutes. Turn the "sandwiches" over and cook for 2 minutes longer. Then transfer them to the prepared baking sheet and place in the oven. Cook for 4 minutes, or until the cheese is melted and bubbly and the chicken is just cooked through. Remove the toothpicks and serve immediately.

4 servings

TURKEY SALTIMBOCCA

Prep time: 12 minutes **Cook time:** 13 minutes **Total:** 25 minutes

Turkey cutlets are available at most groceries today—no pounding needed. That makes it easy! Once browned, the turkey is finished in the oven while you complete the sauce.

. . . .

5 tablespoons olive oil

16 large fresh sage leaves

1 teaspoon salt plus more for seasoning

Eight 4- to 6-ounce turkey breast cutlets

3/4 teaspoon freshly ground black pepper plus more for seasoning

8 thin slices (about 4 ounces) prosciutto

1/2 cup all-purpose flour

1 cup chicken stock or canned, low-sodium chicken broth

1 cup dry white wine

6 tablespoons (3/4 stick) butter, cut into 3 pieces

1. Preheat the oven to 400°F. Line a baking sheet with parchment paper. Place a slotted spoon and a paper towel–lined plate near the stove.

2. Heat 1 tablespoon of the olive oil in an 8-inch sauté pan over medium-high heat. Fry 8 of the sage leaves, in batches if necessary, for about 10 seconds, and then quickly remove them from the pan with the slotted spoon and transfer them to the lined plate to drain. Sprinkle the leaves with a little salt, and set aside. (The leaves will be nicely green and crisp when they have cooled. This can be done a day in advance; keep the fried sage leaves in a closed container at room temperature.)

3. Lay the turkey cutlets on a clean, flat work surface. Season the cutlets on both sides with 1 teaspoon salt and 3/4 teaspoon pepper. Lay one of the remaining (uncooked) sage leaves down the middle of each cutlet, and then roll each cutlet into a tight cylinder. Wrap a slice of prosciutto around each roll.

4. Place the flour in a small shallow bowl, and carefully dredge the turkey rolls in the flour. Set aside.

5. Heat the remaining 4 tablespoons olive oil in a 12-inch sauté pan over medium-high heat. Add the turkey rolls, seam side down, to the pan and brown for 2 minutes. Turn them over and continue to brown on all sides for 2 to 3 minutes longer. Transfer the turkey rolls to the prepared baking sheet (reserve the sauté pan), place it in the oven, and bake for 8 minutes or until the internal temperature registers 165°F on an instant-read thermometer.

6. While the turkey is baking, make the sauce: Add the chicken broth and white wine to the hot sauté pan over medium-high heat. Cook, scraping up any browned bits from the pan, for about 7 minutes or until the liquid is reduced to $\frac{1}{3}$ cup. Whisk in the butter in three separate additions, and remove the sauce from the heat. Season to taste with salt and pepper.

7. Spoon 1 tablespoon of the sauce over each turkey roll, and top each with a fried sage leaf. Serve immediately.

6 to 8 servings

PANKO-CRUSTED CHICKEN TENDERS

Prep time: 15 minutes **Cook time**: 15 minutes **Total**: 30 minutes

A chicken comes with two tenders—one under each breast. In this recipe, you separate the tenders and then cut the rest of the breasts into the tender shape. If you buy chicken breasts that do not include the tender, don't worry; just cut the breast into strips and call them all "tenders."

2 pounds boneless, skinless chicken breasts

1¼ teaspoons salt

½ teaspoon freshly ground black pepper

4 cloves garlic

1 egg

½ cup buttermilk

¼ cup Crystal hot sauce or other Louisiana red hot sauce

2½ cups panko breadcrumbs

½ teaspoon sweet paprika

1¼ cups canola oil or other vegetable oil

1. Remove the tenders from the chicken breasts and place them in a medium-size bowl. Cut the chicken breasts into strips that are similar in size and shape to the tenders, about 1 inch wide and 4 to 5 inches long. Add the chicken strips to the bowl, season with 1 teaspoon of the salt and the black pepper, and mix well to combine.

2. Smash the cloves of garlic with the flat side of your knife. Sprinkle the remaining ¼ teaspoon salt over the garlic, and chop and mash the garlic to form a paste. Transfer the garlic to a medium bowl and whisk in the egg, buttermilk, and hot sauce. Pour this mixture over the chicken pieces and mix well.

3. In another medium bowl or in a gallon-size resealable plastic food storage bag, combine the panko crumbs and paprika. Place half of the chicken pieces in the crumbs and toss to coat evenly. Remove the pieces from the crumbs, shake them lightly, and then transfer them to a small baking sheet or platter. Repeat with the remaining chicken. (The breaded pieces may be stacked on top of one another.)

4. Heat ¾ cup of the canola oil to 350°F in a 12-inch (or larger) sauté pan over high heat. Once the oil is hot, lightly shake loose any excess crumbs from the chicken. Add half of the chicken pieces to the oil, reduce the heat to medium, and cook until the chicken is golden on both sides and just cooked through, 2 to 3 minutes per side. Transfer the cooked chicken to a paper towel–lined plate to drain. Increase the heat under the pan to high, add the remaining $\frac{1}{2}$ cup canola oil, and when it is hot, add the remaining chicken pieces. Reduce the heat to medium and cook the chicken in the same manner. Serve hot or at room temperature.

Note: Panko breadcrumbs are most widely used in Japanese cooking. They are made from crustless bread and create a crispier coating.

4 servings

SLOPPY JOES

Prep time: 10 minutes **Cook time:** 20 minutes **Total:** 30 minutes

A school cafeteria classic that takes me back . . . definitely an oldie but goodie! The Sloppy Joe mixture is even better if left to sit overnight, or for up to three days, in the refrigerator before serving. Or, hey, make a big batch on the weekend and freeze it in airtight containers for busy weeknight meals.

2 tablespoons plus 2 teaspoons olive oil

2 cups diced onions

$1/2$ cup diced celery (small dice)

$1/2$ cup diced green bell pepper (small dice)

1 teaspoon freshly ground black pepper

$3/4$ teaspoon salt

2 teaspoons minced garlic

$1^1/2$ pounds lean ground beef (about 91% lean)

3 tablespoons dark brown sugar

3 tablespoons Worcestershire sauce

2 cups tomato sauce

1 cup beef or chicken stock or canned, low-sodium chicken broth

2 teaspoons hot sauce (optional)

4 to 6 hamburger buns

1. Heat the 2 teaspoons olive oil in a 12-inch sauté pan over medium-high heat. Add the onions, celery, bell pepper, black pepper, and salt, and cook until the vegetables are soft, about 2 minutes. Add the garlic and cook for 1 minute longer. Add the beef, breaking it up with the back of a spoon, and brown for 2 minutes. Then add the brown sugar, Worcestershire, tomato sauce, and beef broth, and bring to a boil. Reduce the heat to a simmer and cook for 15 minutes, stirring as needed. Add the hot sauce if desired, and remove from the heat.

2. While the mixture is cooking, preheat the broiler.

3. Arrange the buns, open-faced, on a baking sheet and lightly brush the cut sides with the remaining 2 tablespoons olive oil. Broil until the buns are golden, about 3 minutes. (Alternatively, grill them in a grill pan or toast them in a skillet, oiled side down, over medium-high heat.)

4. Generously spoon the Sloppy Joe mixture over the toasted bun bottoms. Top with the bun tops, and serve immediately (with forks).

4 to 6 servings

COUNTRY-FRIED STEAK WITH WHITE GRAVY

Prep time: 10 minutes **Cook time:** 30 minutes **Total:** 40 minutes

We've added bacon to this classic home-style dish, and boy, talk about kickin' it up a notch. Serve this alongside the Buttermilk Mashed Potatoes on page 173—they're the perfect vehicle for this rich, creamy gravy and crispy fried steaks. I can taste it now!

8 ounces sliced bacon, cut crosswise into 1/2-inch pieces

1 cup plus 1 1/2 tablespoons all-purpose flour

3 teaspoons Emeril's Original Essence or Creole Seasoning (page 29)

1 large egg

2 to 3 cups milk, as needed

Four 6- to 8-ounce cube steaks

1 1/2 teaspoons salt

1 teaspoon freshly ground black pepper

Vegetable oil, for frying, as needed

1/2 cup minced yellow onion

1. Cook the bacon in a 12-inch sauté pan over medium-high heat until just crisp, about 5 minutes. Remove the pan from the heat. Using a slotted spoon, transfer the bacon to paper towels to drain, leaving the fat to cool in the pan.

2. Combine the 1 cup flour with 1 teaspoon of the Essence in a shallow bowl or pan. Whisk the egg, 1/2 cup of the milk, and 1 teaspoon of the Essence in another shallow bowl or pan.

3. Season the steaks all over with 1 1/4 teaspoons of the salt and 1/2 teaspoon of the black pepper. Dredge the meat in the seasoned flour, then dip in the egg wash, letting the excess drip off, and then dredge in the flour a final time. Set the steaks aside on a tray.

4. Pour the cooled bacon fat into a liquid measuring cup, and add enough vegetable oil to measure 1/2 cup total. Return the mixture to the sauté pan and heat over medium-high heat until it is hot but not smoking. Carefully add 2 of the steaks and fry until golden, 3 minutes per side. Transfer them to paper towels to drain. Add the remaining 2 steaks to the pan, dipping them in the flour one more time before frying if necessary, and cook in the same manner. Transfer the steaks to paper towels.

5. Add the 1½ tablespoons flour to the pan and cook, whisking constantly, for 1 minute. Add the onion and cook, stirring often, until softened, about 3 minutes. Whisk in 1½ cups of the milk, the remaining 1 teaspoon Essence, the remaining ¼ teaspoon salt, and the remaining ½ teaspoon black pepper. Return the bacon to the pan and bring the gravy to a boil. Reduce the heat to medium-low and simmer for 5 to 6 minutes, until the sauce has thickened and there is no raw flour taste. Add additional milk as necessary to achieve the desired consistency.

6. Serve the steaks with the hot gravy.

4 servings

SAUSAGES AND SAUERKRAUT

Prep time: 10 minutes **Cook time:** 21 minutes **Total:** 31 minutes

The type of beer you use here will vary the flavor. If you prefer a slightly bitter flavor to complement your sausage, use a dark or amber beer. A lighter American-style beer will lend a sweeter flavor. Make it with what you like. Make it with what you have! And if you're out of beer, hey, use either more stock or apple cider.

. . . .

One 28-ounce jar sauerkraut, drained

4 ounces sliced apple-cured bacon, cut crosswise into $1/2$-inch pieces

$1\frac{1}{2}$ medium yellow onions, sliced (about 2 cups)

1 tablespoon unsalted butter

$1\frac{1}{2}$ pounds kielbasa or other smoked sausage, cut into 3-inch lengths, casing scored lightly on two sides

2 tablespoons minced garlic

4 fresh thyme sprigs

2 bay leaves

$1/2$ teaspoon coarsely ground black pepper

1 cup chicken stock or canned, low-sodium chicken broth

1 cup beer

1. Place the sauerkraut in a colander and rinse it briefly to remove some of the salt from the brine (don't rinse it too much, or you will lose a lot of the flavor). (Alternatively, if the sauerkraut is not excessively salty, use as is.) Press to release most of the excess liquid, and set aside.

2. Cook the bacon in a large nonreactive skillet or Dutch oven over medium heat for 5 minutes until the fat is rendered. Add the onions and cook for 2 minutes longer. Move the bacon and onions to the side of the skillet and increase the heat to medium-high. Add the butter, and when it has melted, add the sausage. Cook, turning occasionally, until it is browned on both sides and the scores are beginning to open up a bit, 1 to 2 minutes per side.

3. Add the garlic, thyme sprigs, bay leaves, and pepper to the skillet and cook, stirring, for 30 seconds. Add the drained sauerkraut. Toss to combine, scraping up the brown bits that have accumulated in the pan. Add the chicken stock and beer, and bring to a boil. Cover, reduce the heat to a simmer, and cook for 10 minutes.

4. Remove the bay leaves and serve hot.

4 servings

STIR-FRIED BEEF AND BROCCOLI

Prep time: 15 minutes **Cook time:** 12 minutes **Total:** 27 minutes

Once you've assembled the ingredients, this dish goes together like one-two-three. You'll find it easiest to slice the beef in thin strips if it has been partially frozen. And, hey, if you have one very large wok or skillet, this can be done in one batch, cutting the cook time in half. How do you like that!

1/4 cup soy sauce

2 tablespoons minced garlic

4 teaspoons grated fresh ginger

4 teaspoons Chinese black vinegar or balsamic vinegar

3 teaspoons hoisin sauce

3 teaspoons honey

1 1/2 teaspoons crushed red pepper

2 tablespoons cornstarch

4 tablespoons peanut oil

1 large head broccoli, cut into florets

2 pounds beef sirloin steak, thinly sliced across the grain

Steamed white rice, for serving

1. Combine the soy sauce, garlic, ginger, vinegar, hoisin sauce, honey, crushed red pepper, and cornstarch in a small bowl. Mix well, and set aside.

2. Heat a wok or a large skillet over high heat. When it is hot, add 2 tablespoons of the peanut oil and half of the broccoli and cook, shaking the work and stirring frequently, until the broccoli begins to soften, 2 to 3 minutes. Add half of the beef and cook, stirring, for 1 to 2 minutes. Add half of the sauce and stir to evenly coat. Cook until the sauce thickens and the broccoli is crisp-tender, about 1 minute.

3. Transfer to a serving platter and keep warm while you repeat the process with the other half of the ingredients. Serve immediately with steamed white rice.

4 to 6 servings

QUICK AND EASY LAMB KEBABS

Prep time: 15 minutes **Cook time:** 6 to 8 minutes **Total:** 21 to 23 minutes

If you have the time, these simple kebabs can benefit from longer marinating. Why not prep the meat and marinade, set it aside to marinate overnight in the refrigerator, and then pull it out of the fridge the next day and make the kebabs? If you're like me and love a good sauce, these kebabs would be great served with Minted Yogurt Sauce (page 144).

$\frac{1}{4}$ cup plus 1 tablespoon olive oil

2 tablespoons chopped fresh rosemary

2 teaspoons Emeril's Original Essence or Creole Seasoning (page 29)

1$\frac{1}{2}$ pounds boneless lamb (such as leg), cut into 1-inch cubes

2 green bell peppers, cut into 1-inch squares

2 onions, cut into 1-inch pieces

8 large white mushrooms, wiped clean, stems trimmed

8 large cherry tomatoes

Salt and freshly ground black pepper

1. Combine the $\frac{1}{4}$ cup olive oil, rosemary, and Essence in a small bowl. Place the lamb in the bowl and let it marinate while you assemble the remaining ingredients, at least 10 minutes.

2. Arrange the lamb, alternating with the vegetables, on eight 8-inch metal skewers and place them on a large baking sheet. Brush the vegetables with the remaining 1 tablespoon olive oil, and season the skewers on all sides with salt and pepper to taste.

3. Position a rack about 6 inches from the broiler element, and preheat the broiler.

4. Broil the kebabs, turning them once midway, until the meat is well browned, 6 to 8 minutes for medium-rare. Serve hot.

4 servings

THIN-CUT PORK CHOPS WITH ROSEMARY-BALSAMIC GLAZED SHALLOTS

Prep time: 10 minutes Cook time: 15 to 17 minutes Total: 25 to 27 minutes

These quickly seared pork chops are out-of-the-box good when paired with the simple pan sauce. Serve with hot white rice or buttered noodles and a simple vegetable for a complete meal.

Four 6-ounce center-cut pork chops

2 teaspoons kosher salt

1 teaspoon freshly ground white pepper

2 tablespoons Wondra flour (see Note, page 77)

2 tablespoons olive oil

1 tablespoon unsalted butter

1 cup thinly sliced shallots

1 teaspoon minced garlic

1/2 teaspoon chopped fresh rosemary

1/2 cup balsamic vinegar

1 1/2 cups chicken stock or canned, low-sodium chicken broth

1. Season the pork chops on both sides with the salt and white pepper. Dust each pork chop lightly with the Wondra, and set aside.

2. Set a 12-inch cast-iron skillet over medium-high heat, and add the olive oil and butter. When it is hot, place the pork chops in the skillet and sear for 2 minutes per side. Remove the chops from the skillet and set them aside. Add the shallots to the skillet and cook, stirring often, until lightly caramelized, about 2 minutes. Add the garlic and rosemary and cook until fragrant, about 30 seconds.

3. Add the balsamic vinegar and deglaze the skillet. When the vinegar has nearly evaporated (about 1 1/2 minutes), add the chicken stock. Increase the heat to high, and return the pork chops to the skillet. Baste the pork chops with the stock and cook until the liquid has reduced to a sauce consistency, 6 to 8 minutes.

4. Remove from the heat, and serve hot.

4 servings

KICKED-UP SNICKERDOODLES

Prep time: 25 minutes **Cook time:** 14 minutes **Total:** 39 minutes

Everyone loves snickerdoodles! We've sneaked in a bit of cayenne pepper for a surprising little kick.

· ·

2¾ cups all-purpose flour

1 teaspoon baking soda

½ teaspoon salt

½ cup solid vegetable shortening, at room temperature

8 tablespoons (1 stick) unsalted butter, at room temperature

1½ cups plus 5 tablespoons sugar

2 large eggs

1 tablespoon ground cinnamon

¼ teaspoon cayenne pepper

1. Preheat the oven to 350°F.

2. Sift the flour, baking soda, and salt together into a bowl and set aside.

3. In a separate medium mixing bowl, using a hand-held or standing electric mixer, combine the shortening and butter and beat until smooth. Add 1½ cups plus 2 tablespoons of the sugar, and continue beating

until light and fluffy, about 3 minutes. Add the eggs, one at a time, beating well after each addition. Add the sifted flour mixture and mix until the dough just comes together.

4. Combine the remaining 3 tablespoons sugar with the cinnamon and cayenne in a small bowl.

5. Divide the dough into 1½-tablespoon portions and roll them between your hands to form 1½-inch balls. Roll the balls in the spiced sugar. Then divide them evenly among two unlined cookie sheets, spacing them about 1 inch apart. Flatten the balls into ½-inch-thick disks.

6. Bake, rotating the sheets back to front midway, until the edges of the cookies are golden brown, 12 to 14 minutes. Let the cookies cool on the baking sheets on wire racks.

About 30 cookies

SKILLET CORN CAKE WITH STEWED CHERRIES

Prep time: 15 minutes **Cook time:** 25 minutes **Total:** 40 minutes

To make the best use of your time, prepare the deceptively delicious cherry sauce while the corn cake is baking. The cake is best served either warm or at room temperature, with the stewed cherries spooned over the top. Since frozen cherries are available year-round, you'll never need to wait for cherry season to enjoy this dessert.

. . . .

1 cup all-purpose flour

1 teaspoon baking powder

¾ teaspoon salt

6 tablespoons yellow cornmeal

2 large eggs

1 large egg yolk

⅔ cup milk

½ cup olive oil

2 teaspoons grated lemon zest

1½ cups sugar

2 tablespoons unsalted butter

Two 10-ounce bags frozen pitted cherries

¼ cup freshly squeezed lemon juice

1. Place a 10-inch cast-iron skillet in the oven and preheat the oven to 350°F.

2. In a medium bowl, sift together the flour, baking powder, and salt. Stir in the cornmeal.

3. In a separate medium bowl, whisk together the eggs, egg yolk, milk, olive oil, and lemon zest until frothy. Add ¾ cup of the sugar, and whisk to combine. Pour the wet ingredients over the dry ingredients and mix just until the batter is smooth.

4. Swirl the butter in the hot cast-iron skillet until it has melted, and then pour the batter into the skillet. Return the skillet to the oven and cook until the center is set, about 25 minutes.

5. While the cake is baking, set a 10-inch skillet over high heat, and add the cherries, lemon juice, and remaining ¾ cup sugar. Cook until the cherries have released most of their juice, 10 to 12 minutes. Remove from the heat and set aside until ready to use.

6. Allow the cake to cool in the skillet for 5 minutes. Then slice it into wedges and serve with the stewed cherries spooned over the top.

8 servings

60 Minutes
OR LESS

EMERIL'S NEW-STYLE CALDO VERDE

Prep time: 15 minutes **Cook time:** 45 minutes **Total:** 60 minutes

If I had to choose one dish to represent my childhood, it would be this. I call this version "new-style" because the kale is cut into thin strips and is cooked only until crisp-tender, which differs from the more traditional version. Ines, my Portuguese friend back home, would be proud. Serve this with crusty bread alongside.

2 tablespoons olive oil

1½ cups finely chopped yellow onions

1 tablespoon minced garlic

2 pounds Idaho potatoes, peeled and cut into ½-inch cubes

7 cups chicken stock or canned, low-sodium chicken broth

Salt and freshly ground black pepper, to taste

½ teaspoon crushed red pepper

8 ounces kale, large stems and ribs removed

8 ounces firm (smoked) chorizo or other hot smoked sausage, diced or crumbled

½ cup chopped fresh cilantro

¼ cup chopped fresh parsley

2 tablespoons chopped fresh mint

1. Heat the olive oil over medium-high heat in a large soup pot, and add the onions and garlic. Cook until the onions are wilted, 4 minutes. Add the potatoes and chicken stock, cover, and bring to a boil. Season with salt and pepper, and add the crushed red pepper. Reduce the heat to a simmer and cook, uncovered, until the potatoes are tender, 20 minutes.

2. While the potatoes are cooking, thinly slice the kale. Set aside.

3. When the soup is thick and the potatoes have begun to break down, add the sausage and cook for 5 minutes. Stir in the kale and simmer until the leaves have softened but are still slightly crunchy and the flavors have melded, 15 minutes. Stir in the cilantro, parsley, and mint, and season to taste with salt and pepper. Serve hot.

4 to 6 servings

SHRIMP AND CORN CHOWDER

Prep time: 15 minutes Cook time: 35 minutes Total: 50 minutes

This version of a classic Louisiana country soup is simplified by the use of frozen sweet corn, making it easy to cook up year-round. But if fresh local corn is in season when you decide to give this soup a spin, by all means use that instead.

4 tablespoons (½ stick) butter

6 ounces smoked sausage, cut into ¼-inch dice (about 1 cup)

2 cups diced onions (small dice)

1 tablespoon minced garlic

1½ teaspoons salt

1 teaspoon dried thyme

½ teaspoon cayenne pepper

¼ cup all-purpose flour

7 cups shrimp or chicken stock or canned, low-sodium shrimp or chicken broth

1 pound Idaho potatoes, peeled and cut into ½-inch dice (about 2 cups)

3 cups frozen sweet corn

1 pound shrimp, peeled and deveined

½ cup heavy cream

½ cup chopped green onions, white and green parts (optional)

1. Melt the butter over medium-high heat in a 6-quart (or larger) stockpot. Add the sausage and cook until it is browned and the fat is rendered, about 2 minutes. Add the onions and cook until translucent, about 3 minutes. Add the garlic, salt, thyme, and cayenne, and cook for 1 minute.

2. Sprinkle the flour into the pot and cook, stirring often, for 2 minutes.

3. Whisk in the stock, and add the potatoes. Increase the heat to high, cover the pot, and bring to a boil. Uncover, reduce the heat to a simmer, and cook for 15 minutes.

4. Add the corn and cook for 5 minutes. Add the shrimp and heavy cream, and cook until the shrimp is just cooked through, 2 to 3 minutes.

5. Remove the pot from the heat and serve the soup hot, garnished with the chopped green onions if desired.

2½ quarts, 6 servings

CARAMELIZED ONION AND GOAT CHEESE TART

Prep time: 15 minutes **Cook time:** 40 minutes **Total:** 55 minutes

I present to you a tart reminiscent of the French *pissaladière*. (To make this one more authentic, simply replace the cheese with anchovies and top the baked tart with Niçoise olives.) For a twist, you could garnish the tart with toasted pine nuts and fresh figs for an elegant appetizer. Another idea would be to add sautéed spinach. As is or fancied up, this delectable tart is irresistible!

1 egg

¼ cup plus 1 tablespoon water

All-purpose flour, for rolling out puff pastry

1 sheet frozen puff pastry, thawed in the refrigerator

4 tablespoons (½ stick) butter

4 large onions, thinly sliced (about 8 cups)

1¾ teaspoons salt

1¼ teaspoons freshly ground black pepper

4 ounces goat cheese

2 tablespoons chopped fresh basil

1½ teaspoons minced garlic

1½ teaspoons extra-virgin olive oil

1. Line an 11 × 17-inch rimmed baking sheet with parchment paper.

2. In a small bowl, mix the egg and the 1 tablespoon water with a fork.

3. Lightly flour your work surface and roll out the puff pastry to an 18 × 12-inch rectangle (this is more easily done by rolling from corner to corner, on a diagonal, adding more flour as necessary). Transfer the dough to the lined baking sheet. (Another tip: Fold the pastry in half, then, like closing a book, in half again. Unfold it on the baking sheet.) Fold a 1-inch edge toward the center and press it lightly with your fingers to seal it, to form a border along all sides. Brush the edges with the egg mixture. Prick the pastry inside the border thoroughly with your fork. Refrigerate for at least 20 minutes or as long as overnight before baking.

4. Preheat the oven to 400°F.

5. While the pastry is chilling, cook the onions: Melt the butter in a 12-inch skillet over high heat. Add the onions, 1½ teaspoons of the salt, and 1 teaspoon of the pepper, and cook, stirring intermittently, until the onions begin to caramelize, about 10 minutes. Reduce the heat to medium-low and continue to cook, stirring frequently, for 7 minutes. Increase the heat to high, add the ¼ cup water, and stir, scraping up any caramelized bits, and cook for 3 minutes longer. Remove the skillet from the heat, transfer the onions to a small baking sheet, spread them out, and chill in the freezer for 5 minutes.

6. While the onions are chilling, make the filling by combining the goat cheese, basil, garlic, extra-virgin olive oil, remaining ¼ teaspoon salt, and remaining ¼ teaspoon black pepper in a small bowl with a rubber spatula. Set aside until ready to use.

7. Bake the puff pastry in the oven for 5 minutes.

8. Remove the onions from the freezer and stir to help cool them (it's okay if the onions are still somewhat warm). Spread the onions evenly over the pastry. Drop heaping teaspoonfuls of the goat cheese mixture all over the pastry. Return the tart to the oven and bake, rotating it halfway through, until the edges are golden and the cheese has begun to brown, 15 minutes. Serve immediately.

6 to 8 servings

BETTER THAN MAMA'S CHILI-MAC

Prep time: 10 minutes **Cook time:** 40 minutes **Inactive time:** 5 minutes **Total:** 55 minutes

Now *this* is a scrumptious casserole. It is super-simple, and best of all, it's a huge pan of bowl-you-over goodness that will feed the entire family . . . and then some!

. . . .

2 teaspoons olive oil

2 medium onions, cut into small dice (about 3 cups)

2 jalapeños, stemmed and minced (optional)

2 to 3 teaspoons salt, plus more for the pasta water

2 pounds extra-lean ground beef

5 tablespoons Mexican chili powder

1 tablespoon dried Mexican oregano

2 tablespoons minced garlic

One 28-ounce can whole plum tomatoes, broken with your hands, with juices

Two 15-ounce cans kidney beans, drained

1/2 cup water

1 pound elbow macaroni

1 pound medium sharp cheddar cheese

Sour cream, for serving (optional)

1. Heat the olive oil in a 6-quart soup pot over medium-high heat. Add the onions, jalapeños (if desired), and 2 teaspoons of the salt. Cook until the onions are soft, 2 minutes. Add the ground beef, chili powder, oregano, and garlic, and cook, breaking up any clumps of meat with a spoon, for 5 minutes. Add the tomatoes and their juices, beans, and water. Stir, and bring the chili to a boil. Then reduce the heat to a simmer and cook until thickened to chili consistency, about 20 minutes. Taste, and add 1 more teaspoon salt if needed.

2. While the chili is simmering, preheat the oven to 400°F.

3. Place a 9 × 13 1/2-inch or other 3-quart baking dish on a baking sheet. Bring a pot of salted water to a boil, add the macaroni, and cook until just tender, 6 minutes. Drain in a colander, rinse under cool running water, and set aside. Grate the cheddar cheese and set it aside.

4. Once the chili has finished cooking, fold in the cooked macaroni and one-third of the cheddar. Transfer the chili-mac mixture to the baking dish and top with the remaining cheese. Bake until the chili is heated through and the cheese has melted, about 10 minutes.

5. Remove from the oven and let cool for 5 minutes before serving. Garnish each portion with a dollop of sour cream, if desired.

6 to 8 servings

CHICKEN AND MUSHROOM RISOTTO

Prep time: 15 minutes **Cook time:** 31 to 36 minutes **Total:** 46 to 51 minutes

Everyone loves risotto, right? Well, brown some chicken, sauté some mushrooms, and turn a simple risotto into a complete meal.

. . . .

1 pound boneless, skinless chicken thighs, cut into bite-size pieces

1 1/2 teaspoons salt

1 teaspoon freshly ground black pepper

6 tablespoons olive oil

1 shallot, thinly sliced

1 pound shiitake mushrooms, wiped clean, stemmed, and sliced

2 cups Arborio rice

1/4 cup balsamic vinegar

3/4 cup red wine

6 cups chicken stock, or canned, low-sodium chicken broth, heated

2 tablespoons butter

1/2 cup finely grated Parmigiano-Reggiano cheese

1 tablespoon fresh thyme leaves

1. Season the chicken with the salt and pepper, and set aside.

2. Heat 4 tablespoons of the olive oil in a 14-inch sauté pan over medium-high heat. Add the shallot and cook, stirring with a heat-resistant rubber spatula or a wooden spoon, until fragrant and soft, about 1 minute. Add the mushrooms and cook until nicely browned, 3 minutes.

3. Move the mushrooms and shallots to the edge of the pan, and add the remaining 2 tablespoons olive oil. Add the chicken and cook without stirring until browned on one side, 2 minutes. Add the rice and cook, stirring, until the grains are opaque, about 2 minutes.

4. Add the balsamic vinegar and the wine, and continue cooking, stirring frequently, until nearly all of the liquid has been absorbed, 1 minute. Reduce the heat to medium, stir in 3/4 cup of the hot broth, simmer, and stir until nearly all the liquid has been absorbed, about 3 minutes. Continue in this manner, adding more broth, 3/4 cup at a time, and not adding more until the previous addition is absorbed, until all the broth has been added and the risotto is tender and creamy, 20 to 25 minutes.

5. Fold in the butter, cheese, and thyme. Remove from the heat, adjust the seasoning as necessary, and serve immediately.

6 to 8 servings

PORTUGUESE RICE WITH TUNA

Prep time: 10 minutes **Cook time:** 30 minutes **Inactive time:** 5 minutes **Total:** 45 minutes

This moist rice dish is classic Portuguese—it'll knock your socks off. The tuna melts into the flavorful rice along with the onions and peppers and all but disappears. This is a perfect side dish or light entrée when served with a green salad and crusty bread.

1½ tablespoons olive oil

1 medium onion, cut into small dice (about 1½ cups)

1 green bell pepper, cut into small dice (about 1 cup)

3 large cloves garlic, minced (about 1 tablespoon)

1¼ teaspoons salt

¼ teaspoon freshly ground black pepper

¼ teaspoon crushed red pepper

One 14.5-ounce can petite diced tomatoes, drained

One 4.5-ounce can good-quality solid tuna packed in olive oil

1½ cups long-grain white rice

1½ cups chicken stock or canned, low-sodium chicken or vegetable broth

2 tablespoons chopped fresh parsley

1. Heat the oil over medium-high heat in a 4-quart pot. Add the onion and bell pepper and cook until soft, about 3 minutes. Add the garlic, salt, pepper, and crushed red pepper and cook until fragrant, about 1 minute. Add the tomatoes and cook for 4 minutes. Stir in the tuna and its oil, breaking it up with a spoon and mixing well, and cook for 1 minute. Add the rice, stir well to coat, and cook for 1 minute. Stir in the stock and bring to a boil. Cover the pot and reduce the heat to a gentle simmer, and cook until the rice is tender and most of the liquid has been absorbed, 20 minutes.

2. Remove the pot from the heat and let the rice sit, covered, for 5 minutes.

3. Add the parsley and using a fork, gently mix it into the rice, fluffing the rice at the same time. Serve immediately.

6 generous cups, 4 to 6 servings

CHILI-BEANS

Prep time: 15 minutes **Cook time:** 31 to 36 minutes **Total:** 46 to 51 minutes

When they taste it, people will think that this quick-cook chili simmered on the stove all day. Garnish it with the typical suspects if you like—hey, a little cheddar cheese, sour cream, green onions, and jalapeño peppers never hurt anyone!

4 slices thick-cut apple-smoked bacon, diced

2 medium onions, diced (about 3 cups)

$1/2$ red bell pepper, diced (about 1 cup)

$1^1/_2$ pounds lean ground chuck

3 tablespoons Mexican chili powder

2 teaspoons ground cumin

1 tablespoon minced garlic

1 teaspoon dried Mexican oregano

$1^1/_2$ teaspoons salt

One 14-ounce can petite diced tomatoes, with juices

Two 14.5-ounce cans pinto beans, drained and rinsed

One 14.5-ounce can black beans, drained and rinsed

2 cups water

1. Cook the bacon in a heavy Dutch oven over medium-high heat until the fat is rendered and the bacon is crisp, about 5 minutes.

2. Add the onions and bell pepper and cook, stirring occasionally, until the vegetables have softened, about 3 minutes.

3. Add the ground chuck, chili powder, cumin, garlic, oregano, and salt. Cook, stirring occasionally and breaking the meat into small pieces, until the meat is well browned, about 8 minutes.

4. Add the tomatoes with their juices, beans, and water, and bring to a boil. Reduce the heat to a simmer, partially cover the pot, and cook, stirring occasionally, until the meat and beans are tender and the sauce is thick and flavorful, 15 to 20 minutes. Serve hot.

2 quarts, 4 to 6 servings

SEARED SALMON WITH LENTILS

Prep time: 10 minutes **Cook time:** 50 minutes **Total:** 60 minutes

There is something about the combination of salmon and lentils that always makes me come back for more, so I prepare this dish often at home for the family. If you can find French green lentils, get them—they're worth it because they hold their shape well after cooking. Beluga lentils would also work well here. Whatever type of lentil you use, don't overcook them—they should be just tender when you drain them.

9 tablespoons olive oil, plus more for drizzling (optional)

1¼ cups diced red onion (small dice)

½ cup diced celery (small dice)

2 cups French green lentils

8 cups chicken stock or canned, low-sodium chicken broth

1 bay leaf

Salt

Four 6-ounce salmon fillets, skin on

Freshly ground black pepper

1 cup diced red bell pepper (small dice)

¼ cup chopped fresh parsley

3 tablespoons balsamic vinegar

1 teaspoon grated lemon zest

1. Heat 3 tablespoons of the olive oil in a medium saucepan over medium-high heat. When it is hot, add 1 cup of the onion and the celery and cook, stirring, until soft, about 4 minutes. Add the lentils, chicken stock, and bay leaf, and bring to a boil. Reduce the heat to a simmer and cook, uncovered and stirring occasionally, until the lentils are just tender, 35 to 45 minutes. Season to taste with salt, and then drain the lentils in a colander. Set aside while you prepare the salmon.

2. Season the salmon fillets on both sides with salt and pepper to taste. Heat 3 tablespoons of the remaining olive oil in a medium sauté pan over medium-high heat. Place the salmon in the pan, skin side down, and cook until golden brown and crisp, 3 to 4 minutes. Turn the fillets over and cook to the desired degree of doneness, about 2 minutes for medium-rare. Transfer the salmon to paper towels to drain briefly.

3. Transfer the drained lentils to a mixing bowl and add the remaining ¼ cup red onion, the bell pepper, parsley, balsamic vinegar, lemon zest, and the remaining 3 tablespoons olive oil. Toss well to combine, and adjust the seasoning if necessary. Divide the lentils among four wide, shallow bowls, and top each with a salmon fillet. Serve immediately, drizzled with olive oil if desired.

4 servings

ROASTED WHOLE RED SNAPPER WITH ORANGE, ROSEMARY, AND KALAMATA OLIVES

Prep time: 20 minutes **Cook time:** 35 to 40 minutes **Total:** 55 to 60 minutes

I know that there are a lot of you out there who shy away from cooking whole fish at home. But, hey, it's a great technique that leaves you with super-moist, tender fish and delicious pan juices. It's a knockout presentation. Take a walk on the wild side and give this one a try.

Two 3-pound whole red snappers, scaled and gutted

2 tablespoons kosher salt

2 teaspoons freshly ground white pepper

2 large oranges, each sliced into 4 thick rounds

6 sprigs fresh rosemary, plus 2 tablespoons fresh rosemary leaves

1/4 cup julienned orange zest

1/2 cup sliced garlic cloves (1/4-inch-thick slices)

1 cup sliced pitted Kalamata olives

1 1/2 cups dry white wine

1 cup freshly squeezed orange juice

3/4 cup extra-virgin olive oil

1. Preheat the oven to 425°F.

2. Cut 2 parallel diagonal slices, about 3 inches apart and 1/4 inch deep, into each side of the fish. This will make the fish easier to serve. Season the snappers on both sides with the salt and white pepper. Place the orange slices in a large roasting pan, arranging them in two columns of 4 slices each. Place 3 rosemary sprigs across each of the rows of oranges. Lay the fish on top of the orange slices, and scatter the rosemary leaves, orange zest, garlic, and olives evenly over the 2 fish. Pour the wine and orange juice around the

fish, and drizzle each fish with 2 tablespoons of the olive oil.

3. Place the pan in the oven and roast, uncovered, for 20 minutes.

4. Remove the pan from the oven and drizzle 2 more tablespoons of the olive oil over each fish. Return it to the oven and continue to roast until the fish is well caramelized and the flesh flakes easily when tested with a fork, 15 to 20 minutes.

5. Remove the pan from the oven and drizzle the fish with the remaining 4 tablespoons olive oil. Serve immediately, with the pan drippings drizzled over the fish.

Note: To serve the fish, use a large spoon to lift the fish section by section between the diagonal cuts. When the fish from the first side has been served, remove the bone by lifting the tail. Serve the remaining fillets.

4 to 6 servings

BRAZILIAN FISH STEW

Prep time: 25 minutes **Cook time:** 20 minutes **Total:** 45 minutes

The flavors and colors of this dish will wow any seafood lover, trust me. Now, I've gotta tell you, it is a bit on the spicy side, so feel free to reduce the cayenne peppers if you're not a spice lover. With white rice served alongside, this is a complete meal.

. . . .

$2\frac{1}{2}$ pounds red grouper, skin on, scaled and cut into 2-inch pieces (or substitute redfish, flounder, striped bass, escolar, or any other white-fleshed fish)

3 tablespoons freshly squeezed lime juice

$\frac{1}{4}$ cup olive oil

$1\frac{1}{2}$ cups thinly sliced onions

2 to 3 fresh cayenne chiles, stemmed, seeded, and roughly chopped

1 tablespoon minced garlic

2 tablespoons tomato paste

One 14.5-ounce can diced tomatoes, with juices

$\frac{1}{2}$ cup fish or chicken stock, or canned, low-sodium chicken broth, or water

2 teaspoons salt

One 14.5-ounce can unsweetened coconut milk

2 tablespoons chopped fresh cilantro

Steamed white rice, for serving

1. Place the fish in a large nonreactive mixing bowl, add the lime juice, and set aside to marinate while you proceed with the recipe.

2. Heat a large sauté pan over medium-high heat, and add the olive oil. Once it is hot, add the onions and cayenne peppers and sauté, stirring often, until the onions are translucent, 3 to 4 minutes. Add the garlic and sauté for 30 seconds. Add the tomato paste, diced tomatoes, stock, and 1 teaspoon of the salt, and stir well to incorporate. Bring the mixture to a boil. Season the fish with the remaining teaspoon of salt. Then add the fish (with the lime juice) and the coconut milk. Stir to combine, and bring the liquid to a boil. Cover the pan, reduce the heat to medium-low, and cook until the flesh of the fish starts to flake, about 10 minutes.

3. Remove the cover, sprinkle the cilantro over the fish, and serve accompanied by steamed white rice.

6 to 8 servings

SHRIMP ÉTOUFFÉE

Prep time: 16 minutes **Cook time:** 44 minutes **Total:** 60 minutes

Most of the active time here is chopping the vegetables; once the sauce is together, the simmering time leaves you free to do other things. If you have more time available, the sauce can be simmered over low heat for a longer time. This is even better if made a day in advance; simply reheat it gently over low heat.

6 tablespoons (¾ stick) unsalted butter

4 cups chopped onions

2 cups chopped green bell peppers

2 cups chopped celery

2 tablespoons minced garlic

½ cup all-purpose flour

One 14.5-ounce can diced tomatoes, with juices

2 tablespoons Emeril's Original Essence or Creole Seasoning (page 29)

3 cups shrimp or chicken stock or canned, low-sodium shrimp or chicken broth

3 pounds medium shrimp, peeled and deveined

Salt and cayenne pepper, to taste

Steamed white rice, for serving

¼ cup chopped fresh parsley

1. Melt the butter in a large Dutch oven over medium-high heat. Add the onions, bell peppers, celery, and garlic. Cover the pot and cook, stirring occasionally, until the vegetables are tender, 8 to 10 minutes.

2. Add the flour and cook, stirring constantly to pick up the browned bits from the bottom of the pot, until the roux is a golden brown color, 3 to 4 minutes.

3. Add the tomatoes with juices and Essence and continue to cook, stirring, for 2 minutes. Add the stock and bring to a boil. Reduce the heat to a steady simmer and cook until the sauce is thick and flavorful, about 25 minutes.

4. Add the shrimp and cook until they are just cooked through, 2 to 3 minutes. Season with salt and cayenne pepper to taste, and spoon over cooked white rice in wide, shallow bowls. Garnish with the parsley, and serve.

3 quarts, 6 to 8 servings

ROAST TURKEY BREAST WITH BACON AND SAGE

Prep time: 15 minutes **Cook time:** 40 to 42 minutes **Total:** 55 to 57 minutes

When folks tell me that they don't want to fool with roasting an entire turkey, I understand. It can be an undertaking, for sure. But this herbed turkey breast is another thing altogether. It goes together in no time, and the meat ends up incredibly moist and flavorful. I would have no problem whatsoever serving this as the centerpiece of a small Thanksgiving get-together. Just don't skip the bacon!

3 slices thick-cut bacon

1½ tablespoons minced garlic

1 tablespoon chopped fresh sage

1½ teaspoons chopped fresh rosemary

1 teaspoon chopped fresh oregano

1 teaspoon chopped fresh thyme

3 tablespoons unsalted butter, at room temperature

2 teaspoons kosher salt

1 teaspoon freshly ground black pepper

One 2-pound boneless turkey breast, rinsed and patted dry

1. Preheat the oven to 500°F. Line a shallow roasting pan or baking dish with aluminum foil.

2. Cook the bacon in a medium skillet over medium-high heat until crisp, about 6 minutes. Transfer the bacon to paper towels to drain, reserving 1 tablespoon of the rendered bacon fat separately.

3. When the bacon has cooled, chop it fine and transfer it to a small bowl. Add the garlic, sage, rosemary, oregano, thyme, butter, 1 teaspoon of the salt, and ½ teaspoon of the pepper. Using a small spoon, mix thoroughly to combine and form a paste.

4. Using your fingers, gently loosen the skin on both sides of the turkey breast so that it is separated from the flesh. Divide the herb paste in half, and gently spread half between the skin and the flesh on each side of the breast. Season the outside of the turkey breast with the remaining 1 teaspoon salt and ½ teaspoon pepper. Brush the turkey all over with the reserved bacon fat.

5. Place the turkey breast in the prepared pan and roast, uncovered, for 10 minutes. Reduce the heat to 400°F and cook for another 20 to 25 minutes, or until an instant-read thermometer inserted into the deep portion of the breast registers 165°F.

6. Remove the pan from the oven and allow the turkey to rest for 10 minutes before carving it into thin slices. Serve with the pan drippings.

6 to 8 servings

ROAST CHICKEN WITH SHALLOT-GARLIC BUTTER

Prep time: 10 minutes **Cook time**: 45 minutes **Total**: 55 minutes

Everyone needs a good roast chicken in their lives every now and again, and in my family, Sunday dinners are often all about roast chicken. Let's face it, once the chicken is prepped and in the oven, well, as they say, it's all gravy, baby. Take a look at the photos if you've never carved a chicken—it just takes practice, and once you get the hang of it, you can practically do it with your eyes closed.

4 tablespoons unsalted butter, at room temperature

2 tablespoons minced shallot

1 tablespoon chopped fresh parsley

1 teaspoon minced garlic

1 teaspoon salt

3/4 teaspoon freshly ground black pepper

1 whole chicken (about 3 pounds), excess fat and giblets removed, rinsed and patted dry

1. Preheat the oven to 450°F.

2. In a small bowl, combine the butter with the shallot, parsley, garlic, 1/4 teaspoon of the salt, and 1/4 teaspoon of the pepper. Rub 1 tablespoon of the flavored butter on the inside of the chicken, and sprinkle the cavity with 1/4 teaspoon of the salt and 1/4 teaspoon of the pepper. Use your fingers to gently loosen the skin covering the breast, and place 1/2 tablespoon of the flavored butter under the skin on each side of the breast (working from the top end) and under the skin of each thigh (working from the bottom end of the breast). Reserve the extra flavored butter for brushing on the chicken when finished.

3. Tuck the wings behind the bird and tie the leg ends together with kitchen twine. Sprinkle the remaining 1/2 teaspoon salt and 1/4 teaspoon pepper all over the chicken. Set the chicken in a shallow baking dish (just large enough to hold the chicken) and place it in the oven with the legs to the back. Roast for 20 minutes. Baste the chicken with any accumulating juices and roast for 15 minutes longer. Baste the chicken again and roast until the thigh registers 165°F when tested with an instant-read thermometer, 10 to 15 minutes.

4. Transfer the chicken to a cutting board, and let it rest for 10 minutes. Brush the warm chicken with the remaining flavored butter, if desired, then carve and serve with the pan juices spooned over the top.

4 to 6 servings

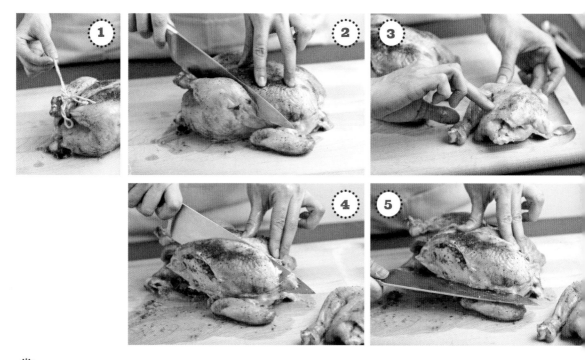

1 After the chicken has rested for at least 10 minutes and has been set on a carving board, remove the kitchen twine.

2 Using a sharp knife, begin to separate the leg and thigh from the breast by slicing between the leg and breast, through the skin, to the joint.

3 To further detach and expose the ball joint, gently pry the leg and thigh away from the breast by pressing it toward your cutting surface. With the tip of your knife, slice through the joint to completely separate the leg quarter. This will involve cutting through to the backbone. Set the leg quarter aside. To separate the leg from the thigh, cut through the joint. If you meet resistance, reposition the knife blade.

4 To remove the breast, slice against the breastbone along the rib. You will have to angle the knife so that the blade runs flat against the ribs (you are not cutting through the ribs; you want to remove the breast from the ribs). Use the tip of your knife to separate the meat from the wishbone.

5 Make another slice along the bottom length of the breast (running parallel to the wing), remove the meat, and set aside. Detach the wing by cutting through the joint. Carve the other side in the same manner.

PORK LOIN WITH APPLES AND PRUNES

Prep time: 10 minutes **Cook time:** 50 minutes **Total:** 60 minutes

This impressive pork roast is a great dish for the fall, when apples are in season at your local farmer's market and you can purchase fresh apple cider. Cozy up to a nice bottle of wine and you're there.

$\frac{1}{2}$ cup dried prunes

$1\frac{1}{4}$ cups fresh apple cider

One $2\frac{1}{2}$-pound boneless pork loin

2 teaspoons salt

1 teaspoon freshly ground black pepper

3 tablespoons olive oil

2 small onions, cut into $\frac{1}{2}$-inch-wide wedges

2 Pink Lady or Honeycrisp apples, peeled, cored, and cut into $\frac{1}{2}$-inch-wide wedges

2 cloves garlic, sliced

$\frac{1}{4}$ cup chicken stock or canned, low-sodium chicken broth

4 fresh thyme sprigs

2 tablespoons cider vinegar

4 tablespoons ($\frac{1}{2}$ stick) cold unsalted butter, cut into small pieces

1. Preheat the oven to 325°F.

2. Place the prunes in a small bowl, add $\frac{1}{4}$ cup of the apple cider, and set aside to soak while you proceed with the recipe.

3. Season the pork loin with $1\frac{1}{2}$ teaspoons of the salt and $\frac{3}{4}$ teaspoon of the black pepper.

4. Heat the oil in a large Dutch oven over high heat. When it is hot, add the pork loin and cook until browned on all sides, 8 minutes. Remove the pork from the pan and transfer it to a baking sheet or platter.

5. Reduce the heat to medium and add the onions, apples, and garlic to the Dutch oven. Cook, stirring occasionally, until caramelized, about 3 minutes. Add the soaked prunes (with any remaining juices) and cook, stirring occasionally, for 3 minutes. Add the remaining 1 cup apple cider and the chicken stock, and bring to a boil.

6. Return the pork loin to the pot, add the thyme sprigs, and bring to a simmer. Cover, and transfer the pot to the oven. Cook, undisturbed, until the pork registers 145°F on an instant-read thermometer, about 30 minutes.

7. Remove the pot from the oven and transfer the pork to a platter. Tent it with aluminum foil to keep warm.

8. Place the Dutch oven over medium-high heat and bring the onion-apple mixture to a boil. Cook until slightly reduced, about 3 minutes. Remove and discard the thyme sprigs. Add the vinegar, remaining ½ teaspoon salt, and remaining ¼ teaspoon black pepper, and stir to combine. While stirring, add the butter, little by little, until it is completely incorporated. Do not allow the sauce to boil or it will separate. Remove from the heat.

9. To serve, spoon some of the sauce onto a serving platter. Slice the pork into thin slices, and arrange them over the sauce. Spoon more sauce over the pork slices, and serve immediately.

4 to 6 servings

GRILLED MARINATED PORK TENDERLOINS WITH AN ORANGE-APRICOT GLAZE

Prep time: 5 minutes **Marinating time:** 20 minutes **Cook time:** 22 to 25 minutes
Total: 47 to 50 minutes

We tested this recipe in a grill pan in our indoor kitchen, but if you're in the mood to fire up the outdoor grill at your house, please, by all means. Your cook time will likely be less, so have your thermometer handy and make sure not to cook the pork beyond 145°F.

$\frac{1}{2}$ cup cider vinegar

6 tablespoons olive oil

2 tablespoons minced garlic

2 pork tenderloins (about 1 pound each)

$\frac{1}{2}$ cup apricot preserves

$\frac{1}{2}$ cup chicken stock or canned, low-sodium chicken broth

1 teaspoon grated orange zest

2 teaspoons salt

1 teaspoon freshly ground white pepper

1. In a 1-gallon resealable plastic food storage bag, combine the vinegar, olive oil, garlic, and pork tenderloins. Seal, and set aside to marinate at room temperature for 20 minutes.

2. While the pork is marinating, prepare the glaze: Combine the preserves, chicken stock, and orange zest in a small saucepan and bring to a boil. Cook until reduced by half, about 5 minutes. Set aside.

3. Set a grill pan over medium-high heat.

4. Remove the pork from the marinade and season it with the salt and white pepper. Place the pork in the hot grill pan and cook for 5 minutes. Turn it over and cook for another 5 minutes. Continue to cook the pork, turning it every few minutes, until it is cooked through, 12 to 15 minutes longer.

5. Remove the pork from the pan and set it aside to rest briefly. Brush with the orange-apricot glaze, slice, and serve hot.

4 servings

PEACH-BLUEBERRY CRISP

Prep time (including topping): 20 minutes **Cook time:** 40 minutes **Total:** 60 minutes

This sinfully delicious crisp can be made any time of the year since it uses frozen peaches and blueberries. Prep it and let it bake while you're enjoying dinner, and it'll be hot and bubbly when you're ready to dive in!

2 teaspoons unsalted butter

One 1-pound bag (4 cups) frozen peaches

One 1-pound bag (3 cups) frozen blueberries

$\frac{1}{2}$ cup sugar

3 tablespoons all-purpose flour

1 teaspoon vanilla extract

Crisp Topping (recipe follows)

Whipped cream, crème fraîche, or vanilla ice cream, for serving (optional)

1. Preheat the oven to 375°F. Grease a 2$\frac{1}{2}$-quart baking dish with the butter.

2. Combine the peaches, blueberries, sugar, flour, and vanilla extract in a large bowl. Toss well to mix. Transfer the fruit to the prepared baking dish, and cover with the topping. Place the baking dish on a parchment- or foil-lined rimmed baking sheet to catch any juices that may bubble over.

3. Bake until the crisp is browned on top and the juices have thickened around the edges, about 40 minutes. Serve with whipped cream, crème fraîche, or vanilla ice cream, if desired.

4 to 6 servings

Crisp Topping

6 tablespoons ($\frac{3}{4}$ stick) cold unsalted butter, cut into small pieces

$\frac{2}{3}$ cup all-purpose flour

$\frac{2}{3}$ cup old-fashioned rolled oats

$\frac{1}{2}$ cup packed light brown sugar

$\frac{1}{4}$ cup packed dark brown sugar

1 teaspoon ground cinnamon

$\frac{1}{2}$ teaspoon finely grated nutmeg

$\frac{1}{4}$ teaspoon salt

Combine all the ingredients in the bowl of a standing electric mixer fitted with the paddle attachment, and process on low speed until the mixture is crumbly and coarse. (Alternatively, combine the ingredients in a bowl, and using a pastry blender, two knives, or your fingers, cut the butter into the dry ingredients until the mixture resembles coarse crumbs.)

Enough topping for 1 crisp

BRAISED CHICKEN THIGHS

Prep time: 5 minutes **Cook time:** 65 minutes **Total:** 70 minutes

When I'm preparing this dish, it's all I can do to wait until it's finished simmering to get a taste of the awesome gravy. You've simply gotta cook some rice to eat with this, no doubt about it.

6 chicken thighs (about 2 pounds), trimmed of any excess skin or fat

1 tablespoon Emeril's Original Essence or Creole Seasoning (page 29)

1 teaspoon salt

1/2 cup plus 1 tablespoon all-purpose flour

2 teaspoons olive oil

3 tablespoons unsalted butter

2 cups thinly sliced yellow onions

1 tablespoon minced garlic

6 sprigs fresh thyme, tied in a bundle, or 2 sprigs fresh rosemary

1/4 teaspoon freshly ground black pepper

3 cups chicken stock or canned, low-sodium chicken broth

1/4 cup chopped fresh parsley

Steamed white rice, for serving

1. Season the chicken all over with the Essence and 1/2 teaspoon of the salt. Place the 1/2 cup flour in a small bowl, and quickly dredge both sides of each thigh in the flour, shaking to remove any excess. Set aside.

2. Heat 1 teaspoon of the olive oil in a 10- to 12-inch flameproof casserole or sauté pan over medium-high heat. Add 2 tablespoons of the butter, and when it has melted, place the chicken, skin side down, in the pan. Brown for 2 minutes on each side. Remove the chicken from the pan and set aside.

3. Add the remaining 1 tablespoon butter to the pan, and when it has melted, add the onions, garlic, thyme bundle or rosemary sprigs, remaining 1/2 teaspoon salt, and the black pepper. Cook, stirring as needed, until the onions are translucent, about 4 minutes. Sprinkle the 1 tablespoon flour over the onions and cook for 2 minutes longer. Then whisk in the chicken stock and increase the heat to high. Return the chicken, skin side down, to the pan, and bring the stock to a boil. Reduce the heat to medium-low, cover the pan with a heavy, tight-fitting lid, and simmer for 15 minutes.

4. Uncover the pan, stir the bottom of the pan to prevent scorching, and turn the chicken skin side up. Cover the pan, and simmer for 20 minutes longer.

5. Stir the bottom of the pan a final time, re-cover, and simmer for 20 more minutes.

6. Remove the pan from the heat and discard the herb bundle or rosemary sprigs. Transfer the chicken to a serving platter. Add the parsley to the sauce, stir to combine, and then spoon the sauce over the chicken. Serve with steamed white rice.

4 to 6 servings

SPINACH AND MUSHROOM LASAGNA

Prep time: 20 minutes **Cook time:** 74 to 78 minutes **Inactive time:** 20 minutes **Total:** 114 to 118 minutes

Though this dish is a bit of a splurge timewise, it is definitely worthwhile. Go on, indulge. As far as lasagna goes, this recipe is actually very simple, and boy, is it delicious. Keep in mind that most of the time is inactive, when the lasagna is either baking in the oven or resting after baking. A great Sunday take-it-to-work-Monday kinda meal.

2 tablespoons olive oil, plus more for the pan

$1\frac{1}{2}$ cups diced onions

1 tablespoon plus 1 teaspoon minced garlic

1 package (about 8 ounces) sliced cremini mushrooms

1 teaspoon salt

10 cups (about 10 ounces) pre-washed fresh spinach, chopped

4 cups your favorite jarred marinara sauce or other tomato sauce for pasta

$\frac{1}{4}$ teaspoon freshly ground black pepper

$1\frac{1}{2}$ teaspoons dried Italian herbs

3 cups low-fat cottage cheese, drained of excess liquid in a strainer

One 8-ounce package no-cook lasagna noodles

12 ounces part-skim mozzarella cheese, shredded (3 cups)

2 cups finely grated Parmigiano-Reggiano cheese

1. Preheat the oven to 375°F.

2. Heat a large nonstick skillet over medium heat, and add 1 tablespoon of the olive oil. Add the onions and sauté until soft and translucent, 3 to 4 minutes. Add the 1 tablespoon garlic and cook for 30 seconds. Then add another $\frac{1}{2}$ tablespoon of the olive oil, the mushrooms, and $\frac{1}{4}$ teaspoon of the salt. Continue to cook until the mushrooms are soft and wilted, 5 to 6 minutes. Remove them from the skillet and set aside.

3. Add the remaining $\frac{1}{2}$ tablespoon olive oil and 1 teaspoon garlic to the same skillet. Add the spinach and sauté, stirring, until wilted, 3 to 4 minutes. Drain the spinach and return it to the skillet. Add the marinara sauce, $\frac{1}{2}$ teaspoon of the salt, the black pepper, and the Italian herbs. Simmer for 3 to 4 minutes. Remove the skillet from the heat and set aside.

4. In a bowl, combine the remaining $\frac{1}{4}$ teaspoon salt and the cottage cheese. Lightly grease a $9\frac{1}{2} \times 13$-inch baking dish with olive oil.

5. Arrange one even layer of lasagna noodles (3 to 4 noodles) in the baking dish so that most of the bottom is covered, taking care that the noodles are not overlapping. Spread a layer of the cottage cheese mixture over the noodles, then top with a third of the mushrooms. Spoon a third of the tomato sauce over all, then top with a third of the mozzarella and a third of the Parmigiano-Reggiano. Repeat the layers two more times, ending with the Parmigiano-Reggiano. Cover the dish with aluminum foil and bake for 45 minutes.

6. Uncover the dish and continue baking until the cheese bubbles and is lightly browned, about 15 minutes. Let the lasagna cool for at least 20 minutes before cutting. Serve hot.

6 to 8 servings

SIMPLE TURKEY MEATLOAF

Prep time: 15 minutes Cook time: 45 to 50 minutes Total: 60 to 65 minutes

My second daughter, Jillian, hasn't eaten red meat since I can remember. She got me started using ground turkey in many things that are typically made with ground beef. Here is an example of one dish that I have come to especially enjoy. And talk about good sandwiches the next day! The perfect accompaniment is, of course, Buttermilk Mashed Potatoes (page 173).

1½ pounds ground turkey, preferably 85/15 blend, or a mix of ground breast and thigh meat

⅔ cup chopped yellow onion

½ cup chopped red or green bell pepper

½ cup unseasoned dry breadcrumbs

⅓ cup chopped celery

1 large egg, lightly beaten

½ cup ketchup

1 tablespoon minced garlic

1 tablespoon Emeril's Original Essence or Creole Seasoning (page 29)

½ teaspoon salt

½ teaspoon freshly ground black pepper

1 tablespoon hot sauce

1. Position a rack in the center of the oven and preheat the oven to 375°F.

2. Place the turkey in a large mixing bowl. Add the onion, bell pepper, breadcrumbs, celery, egg, 1 tablespoon of the ketchup, the garlic, Essence, salt, and pepper. Mix gently but thoroughly until the ingredients are well combined. Transfer the turkey mixture to a 1-pound loaf pan, and form it into a domed loaf shape.

3. Place the remaining ketchup in a small bowl, and stir in the hot sauce. Spoon the ketchup mixture evenly over the meatloaf, spreading it with the back of a spoon.

4. Bake until the meatloaf is browned on top, cooked through, and an instant-read thermometer inserted into the center registers 165°F, 45 to 50 minutes.

5. Remove the pan from the oven and let the meatloaf rest for 5 minutes before serving.

4 to 6 servings

Index